DANCING WITH THE LAW

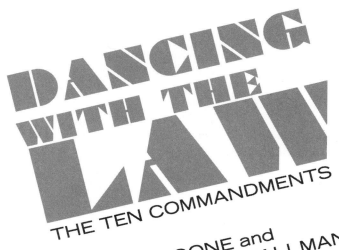

DANCING WITH THE LAW

THE TEN COMMANDMENTS

DAN BOONE and
AMY BOONE TALLMAN

BEACON HILL PRESS
OF KANSAS CITY

ISBN 978-0-8341-2491-2

Printed in the
United States of America

Cover design: J.R. Caines
Interior design: Sharon Page

Library of Congress Cataloging-in-Publication Data

Boone, Dan, 1952-
    Dancing with the law : the Ten commandments / Dan Boone and Amy Boone Tallman.
        p. cm.
    Includes bibliographical references.
    ISBN 978-0-8341-2491-2 (pbk.)
    1. Ten commandments—Criticism, interpretation, etc. 2. Bible. O.T. Exodus XX, 1-20—Criticism, interpretation, etc. I. Tallman, Amy Boone, 1977- II. Title.

    BV4655.B645 2010
    241.5'2—dc22

                                                                    2009044140

10 9 8 7 6 5 4 3 2 1

CONTENTS

ACKNOWLEDGMENTS

Dan's

Those who teach us to respect the boundaries are our friends. They may be parents, pastors, coaches, or mentors—but they care about us.

I have been blessed to have such people in my life. And in this book, I'd like to single out the people of Trevecca Nazarene University. Before I was born, they affected my parents through their compassion for a needy family and their welcome to a young married couple. I grew up knowing that my college was Trevecca. Never a doubt. I honestly didn't know there were other options. I would not have been as wise in choosing a college as those who chose for me. In letting me leave McComb, Mississippi, my parents were releasing me from their proximity to serve God wherever. Now that I have three children, I respect my parents' choice even more. They seemed to know that my future was somehow wrapped up in the people who would form me during my college years. They were right. At Trevecca, I met the joy of my life, Denise, and together we formed friendships that are so close to the surface of our life today that it only takes minutes of conversation to be back where we were then. Professors shaped me, administrators knew my name, friends were true, and I was loved. I wish every young adult could experience what I did on the Trevecca campus. It might do wonders for our world.

Looking back I realize that Trevecca was legalistic in some ways, but I've long since left that in the rearview mirror. I hope you have too. But the core of that legalism, the true intent of those who aim to follow God's law to the letter, still holds—an experience of devotion to God and concern for neighbor that is reflected in a daily life of holiness. And now, thirty-five years after graduating, I am back as Trevecca's president. I walk the hill with gratitude for what was instilled in me by those good people. I will not start naming them because they are legion.

And as I watch the next generation of believers taking shape at Trevecca, I am hopeful for the world. They aren't legalistic, but they also don't seem to mind when I talk about the boundaries of the holy life that identify the people of God. In fact, they seem more willing than my own generation to make sacrifices according to God's law. Where my generation held the law up, this generation holds it close. This generation believes that the law of God is part of life, and that doesn't scare them or frustrate them; it empowers them. We know amazing things can happen because of God's law. The planet can be restored, marriage can work, wrongs can be righted, and peace can prevail. I've raised three daughters in this generation, one of whom helped me write this book, and two of whom attended Trevecca. I'm confident that a love for God's law is being instilled in them and in others of their generation all across the world at churches, in small groups, at family dinners around the kitchen table, and at institutions like Trevecca Nazarene University. And this world will change for the better because of it.

Amy's

I've dreamed about this day for a long time—writing my first acknowledgments in a book with my name on the cover. I always knew that God would be the first person I'd thank and credit. That part was easy. I am indebted to my Creator, and I am deeply in love with Him, so thanking Him comes naturally.

But I've got another father to thank. I have been so blessed to work on this book with my father. Let's face it, my dad, Dan Boone, is the brains behind this operation. He can tell you what the Hebrew translation is; I can tell you why it's still a dangling modifier. He's the theologian; I'm the writer, or at least that's who our diplomas tell us we are. But I think there is something profound about the coming together of a university president and a stay-at-home mom to write a book about God's law. In our society, the power (and pay) divisions between a university president and a stay-at-home mom are, well, vast. But God keeps reminding me that we all have work to do. Just as my dad seeks to follow God's law as he leads thousands of students and employees at Trevecca Nazarene University, I'm seeking to shape my two young daughters, Eleanor and Clara, into little law-lovers. And we are both leaning on the One who handed down tablets of chiseled stone to get us through each day.

The Ten Commandments, God's law, is meant for all of us, right where we are. But presidents and moms alike should be warned. Just because God's law is for everyone everywhere doesn't mean God will leave us how or where He finds us. His law is too good at moving us. *(Cue the music.)*

THE TEN COMMANDMENTS
(Exod. 20:1-20)

Then God spoke all these words:

I am the LORD your God, who brought you out of the land of Egypt, out of the house of slavery; you shall have no other gods before me.

You shall not make for yourself an idol, whether in the form of anything that is in heaven above, or that is on the earth beneath, or that is in the water under the earth. You shall not bow down to them or worship them; for I the LORD your God am a jealous God, punishing children for the iniquity of parents, to the third and the fourth generation of those who reject me, but showing steadfast love to the thousandth generation of those who love me and keep my commandments.

You shall not make wrongful use of the name of the LORD your God, for the LORD will not acquit anyone who misuses his name.

Remember the sabbath day, and keep it holy. Six days you shall labor and do all your work. But the seventh day is a sabbath to the LORD your God; you shall not do any work—you, your son or your daughter, your male or female slave, your livestock, or the alien resident in your towns. For in six days the LORD made heaven and earth, the sea, and all that is in them, but rested the seventh day; therefore the LORD blessed the sabbath day and consecrated it.

Honor your father and your mother, so that your days may be long in the land that the LORD your God is giving you.

You shall not murder.

You shall not commit adultery.

You shall not steal.

You shall not bear false witness against your neighbor.

You shall not covet your neighbor's house; you shall not covet your neighbor's wife, or male or female slave, or ox, or donkey, or anything that belongs to your neighbor.

When all the people witnessed the thunder and lightning, the sound of the trumpet, and the mountain smoking, they were afraid and trembled and stood at a distance, and said to Moses, "You speak to us, and we will listen; but do not let God speak to us, or we will die." Moses said to the people, "Do not be afraid; for God has come only to test you and to put the fear of him upon you so that you do not sin."

INTRODUCTION:
DANCING WITH THE LAW

How do you feel about law? When's the last time you browsed the two-volume truth-in-lending law or the federal law for income tax or the rule book at your local school? I would guess if you requested to see a copy of your company code book, the pages would be in pristine condition, hardly thumbed by human fingers. Have you ever known anyone to record the company policy manual on a CD so he or she could memorize it en route to and from work? Or have you ever come across a college student sprawled out in the middle of campus reviewing the campus code of conduct?

We don't turn to law on normal days—only when we are violated and want to use it to our benefit or when we are in trouble and wish to challenge its unpleasant ruling on our behavior. Law is big words in unused books for hard situations that we hope to never find ourselves in.

For most of us, the words surrounding law are not our favorites—*rule, restriction, regulation, requirement, code, commandment, covenant, limit, boundary, must, ought, shall, will.* These are parental words, court words, conflict words. So we use them only when we have to; otherwise, we hold them at a distance.

The Israelites had a different take on law. They took their copy of the law their God had given them, clutched it to their chests, and danced with it. They celebrated it as a gift. They observed it daily in their relationships and required their young to memorize it. And when a copy of the law had grown ragged and old, they had a special ceremony to retire it. They buried it with all the dignity of a beloved grandparent's body.

But don't take my word for it. Listen to parts of the longest psalm in our Scriptures and note the numerous ways these people lavish praise on the gift of law. I've only included excerpts of it here because this text is so long. But for this opening chapter to really take hold, I suggest you open your Bible and actually read the entire chapter of Ps. 119. The weight of love for the law in this text is absolutely stunning.

Teach me, O LORD, the way of your statutes,
    and I will observe it to the end.
Give me understanding, that I may keep your law
    and observe it with my whole heart.
Lead me in the path of your commandments,
    for I delight in it.
Turn my heart to your decrees,
    and not to selfish gain.
Turn my eyes from looking at vanities;
    give me life in your ways.
Confirm to your servant your promise,
    which is for those who fear you.
Turn away the disgrace that I dread,
    for your ordinances are good.
See, I have longed for your precepts;
    in your righteousness give me life.
. . . .
Oh, how I love your law!
    It is my meditation all day long.
Your commandment makes me wiser than my enemies,
    for it is always with me.
I have more understanding than all my teachers,
    for your decrees are my meditation.
I understand more than the aged,
    for I keep your precepts.
I hold back my feet from every evil way,
    in order to keep your word.

I do not turn away from your ordinances,
  for you have taught me.
How sweet are your words to my taste,
  sweeter than honey to my mouth!
Through your precepts I get understanding;
  therefore I hate every false way.
Your word is a lamp to my feet
  and a light to my path.
I have sworn an oath and confirmed it,
  to observe your righteous ordinances.
I am severely afflicted;
  give me life, O LORD, according to your word.
Accept my offerings of praise, O LORD,
  and teach me your ordinances.
I hold my life in my hand continually,
  but I do not forget your law.
The wicked have laid a snare for me,
  but I do not stray from your precepts.
Your decrees are my heritage forever;
  they are the joy of my heart.
I incline my heart to perform your statutes
  forever, to the end.

. . . .

Your decrees are wonderful;
  therefore my soul keeps them.
The unfolding of your words gives light;
  it imparts understanding to the simple.
With open mouth I pant,
  because I long for your commandments.
Turn to me and be gracious to me,
  as is your custom toward those who love your name.
Keep my steps steady according to your promise,
  and never let iniquity have dominion over me.

Redeem me from human oppression,
    that I may keep your precepts.
Make your face shine upon your servant,
    and teach me your statutes.
My eyes shed streams of tears
    because your law is not kept. *(Vv. 33-40, 97-112, 129-35)*

Now how do you feel about law? When we feel like the psalmist of Ps. 119, I think we will have come to understand it the way the people at the time did—as a sacred gift that points the way to the life God intended for us. And this gift comes to us in the setting of a story, *our* story.

God's relationship with us does not begin with the Ten Commandments but in a garden with a handful of directives, rules, and laws: tend the garden, name the animals, hands off the tree in the center of the garden. But how quickly the laws are tossed aside. Desiring to be our own rulers, to be like God, to give orders rather than receive them, we violated the arrangement. We broke the law. Before we get to page 3 of our garden story, we are pointing fingers, covering up, hiding, and murdering. It gets worse, with evil exponentially covering the earth. Then the Flood comes. Our response to the enormous judgment of water is to build a tower of Babel to have high ground should God come after us again with a deluge.

Fast-forward to Abraham, Isaac, Jacob, and Joseph—recipients of grand promises about land and blessing and future generations. There are plenty of stories that suggest the faithfulness of God to the first three as they journeyed in a mode of trust. And then Joseph lands in Egypt, first as a slave and eventually as second in command to Pharaoh.

After four hundred years in Egypt, a pharaoh comes to the throne with no memory of the great Joseph, savior of Egypt during the famine. This new breed of pharaoh can count well enough to surmise that we—the descendants of Joseph and his family—are numerous and pose a threat to his empire. He begins to treat us like slaves, which makes us feel like slaves.

Our people are corralled in Goshen, the mud pit city of the brick-making industry. Pharaoh rarely makes it down to Goshen, but his law frequents the place. He barks out orders from his fancy throne. More bricks. Less straw. No vacations. No unions. No time off. And anytime we make a request, he figures we've got too much time on our hands and ups the brick quota. Life in Goshen is drab. There is little singing and dancing, and even less laughter. We are stuck. We tramp straw in mud all day long. We sleep with Goshen dirt under our toenails. And no one on the planet gives a rip about us. No one knows or remembers us—except God.

Late at night when no one else can hear our cries, God does. Late at night when no one else can see our tears, God does. When we're lying on mats (or on our king-sized pillow top mattress), thinking how utterly trapped we are, how helpless we feel, how monotonous our daily routine is, how inhumane we are treated, how used we are—God comes.

Our God does not sit on a plush throne in heaven and bark out new orders for the folk in Goshen. Our God comes down to earth in bushes that burn. Our God comes in rivers that turn red, frogs in Pharaoh's bed, gnats in Pharaoh's bread, flies on Pharaoh's head, cows that turn up dead, boils bright red, locusts determined to be fed, and darkness full of dread. Our God comes down to Goshen, because God does not like what Pharaoh has done to us. God shreds Pharaoh's old slave employee manual, beats him ten out of ten plagues, and makes him cry uncle, mercy. There is a dark night of death, in which a mysterious meal is eaten and blood is smeared on the wood of the doorpost. And the next morning, we are free to leave. Did we hear that correctly? Free to leave?

Freedom—it's a sigh of relief, but we have to be very careful with that word. Everybody serves somebody. If freedom is the end of the story for the people of God, then the Exodus story is done. Roll the credits: Moses—Charlton Heston, collapsing sea—courtesy of SFX, Sound—Dolby.

Not so fast. We are lousy at being our own boss. Multiply freedom times every liberated slave and you get thousands of self-governing Jews running around calling the shots. Individual freedom is impossible unless everyone in the universe is willing to bow to the desires of one. We do not know how to live free. And our creation as relational beings suggests that personal freedom is not the epitome of life, nor is it the goal of the Creator. Even the Creator is known as a community called Trinity in which each member lovingly serves the interests of the other. Each yields to, glorifies, is united with, and moves in harmony with the other.

Our story continues. We are moving away from Pharaoh with the goods of Egypt bulging in our pockets. At the sea (a place reminiscent of the time we were spared in Noah's genes), we are threatened by Pharaoh, who doesn't let us go without one last fight. God moves in the same breath that created the earth and dried Noah's flood-soaked land, and makes a way for us where there is no way. We walk on dry ground to our freedom, and Pharaoh meets the fate of earlier flood victims.

We travel through the wilderness waiting for God to tell us every move. Camp here. Go there. Eat this. Drink this. We are free; God provides, but still we gripe like slaves. Apparently, in Egypt we perfected the art of making someone else responsible for our misery. "What, no water? I'm sick of manna. The food in Egypt was better than this! What are you trying to do, Moses? Bring us out here in the wilderness and kill us all? It would have been better to have died in Egypt." Moses got so fed up with us that he questioned God, "Why have *You* burdened me with *these* people?" We're well past Pharaoh, but we are griping, directionless, self-centered, demanding, going nowhere.

One day God announces to Moses (I think I hear a firm intention in God's voice), "Get the people ready. In three days I'm going to meet with them on Mount Sinai. Consecrate them and have them wash their clothes, and as far as sex goes for the next three days—don't even think about it. Set limits around the mountain. Anyone who crosses the line and touches the holy mountain will die. Only after the trumpet blast signals you that it's safe can you approach the mountain" (see Exod. 19).

We didn't go near the mountain. It was covered with a thick cloud. Lightning was splitting trees, and thunder was shaking the ground beneath our feet. The mountain was on fire, smoking like a chimney. Moses turned to us and said, "Let's go meet God." Nobody moved. Moses was the only soul willing to venture forth. I suppose he wasn't stunned by this display of divinity; it had been on this very spot that God had spoken to him from a burning bush and given him his life's work. Fire, thick clouds, thunder, and lightning—this was the God that Moses knew. The two of them had a conversation that resulted in us staying at the foot of the mountain while Moses became our ears at the top of the mountain. When Moses came down, we heard the words of God: "I am the Lord your God, who brought you out of the land of Egypt, out of the house of slavery" (Exod. 20:2) and the commandments followed.

God introduced himself to us as the God who brought us "out of the land of Egypt, out of the house of slavery." He had earlier introduced himself to Moses as the God of our fathers Abraham, Isaac, Jacob, and Joseph. What kind of God is this who makes himself known by what He does? The name of this God is defined by action. This God can be known in a bush, a plague, an opened river, a shower of manna, a pillar of fire, an etched stone, and a glowing face. This God travels. This God is experience-able. This God communicates. This God is like no other god, which is the same as saying "holy." This God means to be taken seriously.

Something happened to us that day at that mountain that has left an indelible impression on us, and all at once, we knew. We knew we had been delivered by a power greater than any other power in heaven or on earth. We knew that with His own finger, God had inscribed the way of life for us. We knew that autonomy and self-rule was the last thing on this God's mind. We knew that we were saved into a serious life of obedience. We knew that this relationship with God had expectations. We knew that other gods would try to seduce us and lay claim to us, and this was verboten. We knew that it mattered to God how we treated each other—our servants, our spouses, our parents, our children, our neighbors, and the strangers who came within our gates. We knew that concern for another's property mattered to this God.

Our response was shaky:

When all the people witnessed the thunder and lightning, the sound of the trumpet, and the mountain smoking, they were afraid and trembled and stood at a distance, and said to Moses, "You speak to us, and we will listen; but do not let God speak to us, or we will die." Moses said to the people, "Do not be afraid; for God has come only to test you and to put the fear of him upon you so that you do not sin." Then the people stood at a distance, while Moses drew near to the thick darkness where God was. *(Exod. 20:18-21)*

The law giving continued for several chapters in our story before there is any real response on our part. Finally in Exod. 24:3, we are heard to say, "All the words that the LORD has spoken we will do."

Fast-forward past that day at the foot of the smoking mountain. Our word proved fickle. Sometimes we did what we said we would do. Sometimes we didn't. There are exile stories about the times we didn't obey the commands of the Lord. When we were captives again, this time in Babylon, our memories of Egypt were evoked in a book called Exodus. The retold story reminded us

18

how we got ourselves into slavery—disregard for the commands of God. Our sixth-century B.C. retelling of the thirteenth-century B.C. event reminded us that our God still has the power to hear cries, overthrow powers, and liberate slaves. But this God means to be taken seriously.

More time has passed since the days of exile. Our promises are still fickle. We have stood once again at the foot of a holy mountain. This one is called Golgotha. We saw the Holy One hanging on a tree under the judgment of every pharaoh. The sky darkened and thunder rumbled. He had come to Goshen and Goshen had crucified Him. There was blood smeared on wood again. A lamb died to take away the sin of the world.

In a move reflective of Exodus, God raised Jesus from the dead and gave to us the gift of His risen Spirit. In this act, the law of God is written, not on tablets of stone, but on our hearts. We are given the capacity to be faithful, not fickle. We are empowered to keep the law as an expression of wise gratitude for the gift of a way of life defined in the law. The Word becomes flesh. Jesus becomes for us the definition of the law. Everything the law says, Jesus is.

And because it's easier to dance with a person than a stone tablet, we join the people of Ps. 119 in joyous, reflective gratitude for a way of life made possible by the One who is for us the way, truth, and life. Because somewhere, some free child of God is saying a firm *no* to other gods. Some redeemed child of God is being restored by keeping the Sabbath. Some liberated soul is honoring a parent. Somebody is deciding against abortion. Somebody is telling the truth. Somebody is walking away from a flirtatious temptation. Somebody is respecting another's property. It is the way of life embodied in Jesus. And if that's not worth dancing about, I don't know what is. So go ahead. Hug the law tightly; give the law a twirl. Let's dance!

1

PROMISED LAND—
HERE OR THERE?

In the story of Exodus, something divine happens. Something that is inexplicable apart from the activity of God. This happening becomes the formative story of the Jews. This story shapes the nationalistic desires of their nation even to this day. It shapes their very beliefs. They believe they are the chosen people of their God. They believe that in their weakness, God is strong. They believe that a powerless nation can overcome a stronger political entity. They believe that their existence is somehow tied up in the will of this God. They believe that they are the light to the Gentiles and that their Jerusalem is the hill to which these Gentile nations will one day stream to bow in worship of God. They believe that God can grow weary of their lawlessness and exile them among pagans but cannot forget them and will, sooner or later, bring them home to the land promised—their Middle Eastern turf. These beliefs drive their understanding of land rights, political power, and foreign relations. All this is rooted in Exodus.

The Exodus story is also formative for Christians. God acts and something inexplicable happens. Slaves are set free. The powerless are empowered for a journey thought impossible. The powerful are left in shambles with their firstborns in the mortuary and their army at the bottom of the sea. God rewrites the expected ending. The dying live; the living die. In essence, Christians see the shadow of resurrection in this story. God moves in a way that creates a future where there was none. A dead end becomes a new highway. People without need for a map now browse travel brochures. They are going somewhere. Their future is blessed by God. Tomorrow is a gift.

Out of this come the Ten Commandments. They come on the other side of Egypt, on the other side of liberation. They are not given as an exit plan from Egypt or a road map to the Promised Land. They are given after God has already acted on their behalf. The commandments are given to people who used to be as good as dead and are now vibrantly alive—and free.

Until we get it fixed in our hearts and minds that law is not how we get to God, earn God, gain God's attention, placate or impress God, we will not understand the place of the law in our lives. Law is simply how the redeemed live.

And that law is given for life on earth. Sometimes I think we forget that the Ten Commandments were given to God's people who were en route to an earthly place. We fondly call their destination the Promised Land. God had made promises to Abraham about land. That promise stayed alive and gave them something to hope for, even in the mud pits of Goshen. But their hopes were not that they would one day die and leave filthy old Egypt behind and go to heaven where the streets were gold and the angels played harps and nobody bossed you around anymore. They hoped for earthly turf where they could work the land, raise a family, and worship God. But we Christians have turned the Promised Land into an unearthly place out in the galaxy somewhere. Flip through the hymnal and listen to our wishful longing for a faraway land. In our songs we talk about a promised land, flowing with milk and honey. We say that we are just passing through this world on our way to Glory Land, Sweet Beulah Land.

I do understand the longing behind these lyrics. I've sung these songs with a wistful longing to be freed from the earthly burdens of labor, sickness, trouble, and death. I do not mean to minimize the desire to be away from the effects of a sinful world, beyond the reach of evil and its consequences. Every child of God feels this tug at some point. And those who have more friends and family on the other side of death feel it especially strong. This is not a denial of the blessed reality of heaven. It is, however, an attempt to deliver us from an escapist faith that embraces a future beyond this world rather than embracing the future of a kingdom coming to this world in a glorious act of bodily resurrection, planetary restoration, and global justice.

If we desire a rest from our labor in the presence of God, the law addresses this in the commandment about Sabbath. But if we think the law is a list of things to do to get to heaven, we have missed its intended function as a way of life on earth. God's primary interest is not to get us to heaven but to get heaven in us on earth. Remember this part of the Lord's Prayer, "thy will be done in earth, as it is in heaven" (Matt. 6:10, KJV). The Promised Land is the land beneath our feet right now, where the God who liberates the captive and raises the dead seeks to bless us with a way of life that is rich in mercy, justice, and righteousness.

Sadly, many of us have given up on much happening here on earth. Like the Jews tramping straw in Pharaoh's mud pits, like the slaves on the southern cotton plantations, like the elderly woman watching nonstop TV news, we've set our sights on escaping to another world. We no longer believe that our eyes will see God's redemption in the land of the living.

We forget that our own scriptures speak of the earth as the site of God's last great redemptive move. We forget that the heavenly city is coming down to earth. We forget that we are not going to where God is but that God is coming to where we are. We forget that the risen Jesus tells His disciples to meet Him, not just inside the Eastern Gate, but on the road to Galilee. We forget that the ultimate hope of the Christian is not that our soul would ascend to heaven but that our body would be raised from an earthly grave. We forget that Paul's great chapter on the resurrection of Jesus ends, not with "Thank God, we're all going to heaven," but "Be steadfast, immovable, always excelling in the work of the Lord, because you know that in the Lord your labor is not in vain" (1 Cor. 15:58).

The Ten Commandments are not a list to observe so we can go to heaven someday. They are the gift of heaven already landed in our hearts by the God who gives life to His redeemed—which means that the Ten Commandments are better understood as a corporate instruction for the formation of a people, rather than a list of personal morals to be observed. Every commandment is highly relational, reflecting the way we relate to God—worship no other gods, make no images, do not misuse God's name; and reflecting the way we relate to each other—honor your parents, be faithful to your spouse, do not murder, do not steal. You can't keep a single commandment by yourself. Obedience requires another; even if he or she is the person you don't envy or kill.

Maybe we are wrong to insist that the Ten Commandments remain the ethical code for a pluralistic society. Only God followers can keep the first three commandments, and the only way they can keep them is by virtue of the Spirit dwelling in them, writing the law on their hearts and empowering them to obey it. To demand this of pagans is to demand the impossible and the unlikely. Granted, the last six commandments may have principled wisdom to guide lawmaking and life in community, but if these are separated from the narrative of the first four commandments, the very likeness of God that defines behavior toward our fellow humans is lost. The God we worship in the first four commandments is the God who

- creates respecting families (think Trinity as a loving community)
- loves life more than murder (think Jesus' words to a sword-slinging Peter in the Garden of Gethsemane)
- cherishes marital faithfulness as an example of His treatment of His own covenanted bride (think the prophetic calls for a wayward bride to return to her faithful, suffering covenant partner)
- respects the boundary of bodies not to be used without permission (think Virgin Mary)
- respects property (think instructions to the Ephesians to steal no longer but to work with the hands and supply gifts to the needy)
- calls for truth to be spoken (think Jesus' words before Pilate)

- covets nothing (think Jesus emptying himself and becoming a servant who grasped for nothing but the Father's will)

The commandments are a three-chapter narrative that flows

from God

to

deliverance

to

God-worship

to

God-like behavior.

You can't break into the narrative and expect the God-like behavior without the prior saving activity of God. This is not a checklist. It's a story of people being transformed. And it's our story.

2
BY WHAT AUTHORITY?

On July 18, 1996, an early morning Bible-quoting contest turned ugly in Dadeville, Alabama, ending with one man dead and another fleeing justice. Gabel Taylor, 38, died after being shot in the face. Police are looking for a suspect who was comparing his Bible knowledge with Taylor's. It was discovered that their disagreement arose because they were quoting different versions of the same passage. The suspect reportedly retrieved his Bible and was angered when he discovered that he had been wrong.

True story. And as sad as this account is, it is not the first time a believer has sought to defend his or her interpretation of Scripture with an angry tirade. We live in a chapter of the Christian story in America that finds many people defending the authority of Scripture in ways that do great damage to the cause of God and the people for whom Christ died. They are the kind of Christians we wouldn't want to be linked to. Could it be they misunderstand the issue at stake?

As I read about the frighteningly awesome theophany (encounter with God) in Exod. 19, I have a hard time believing that God needs humans to come to His rescue. Someone would have to be a fool to mess with the God of a smoking mountain and thundering voice. I doubt Moses put a boundary around the mountain to protect God from people who would harm Him. God does not need humans rising in anger to take on those who suggest alternative ways of interpreting the Bible. God is not shaking in His boots over what we may say about Scripture. God does not shrink in the face of opposition. In short, God can handle His own battles.

However, many interpret such behavior as an act of loyalty on their part. This God who liberated them is precious; therefore, they defend any attack against His honor or truthfulness. But how? By shooting someone? By destroying them in a theological tirade? By firing them? How does Scripture instruct us to deal with them? If we are to respond to our enemies the way God responds to His enemies, we will lay down our lives for them. We will love them as God loves them. And we will speak truth in love, seeking to correct, but not to show off our knowledge or our angry power.

But the issue goes much deeper than this. When someone defends the authority of Scripture, what is he or she defending? The words in the Bible? The authority of the Bible to tell us how to order our lives? The unchangeableness of the text? A specific interpretation of the words of Scripture? What are we defending? And does it really need to be defended?

The Bible suggests that authority does not reside in words but in persons. In other words, the most important thing about the Ten Commandments is not necessarily what they say but who spoke them into being—God! The authority of Scripture is not the issue. The issue is the authority of the God who speaks to us in the Scriptures. The book itself bears no innate authority apart from the God whose Spirit is at work in and through the reading of the book. God is authority personified.

We catch a glimpse of this in the Sermon on the Mount. Jesus speaks to religious leaders and common folk about the new reign of God that is breaking in on them in His teachings. Matthew 5 contains a text about the fulfillment of words from the law and prophets. They are meant to be fulfilled, not defended. Lived out, not debated. Embodied, not protected. At the conclusion of the sermon, the response of the people is astonishment, because He taught them, not as one of the scribes, but as one having authority. Authority rests in the people who speak, not in the words they speak.

Authority, in the Exodus story, is the ability to deliver slaves from Pharaoh's grasp, to part the sea, and to make manna fall from heaven. In the newer testament it is the power to heal the blind, to forgive sin, to feed a multitude, to raise the dead. Authority is not about proving whether or not something happened, or whether it is scientifically verifiable, or whether the dating sequence is correct, or whether or not it was written by Paul. We have invested ourselves in making biblical authority a matter of human debate and defense. The best way to demonstrate the authority of Scripture is to know and be transformed by the God who is revealed in Scripture. Sadly, the debate over the authority of Scripture has sunk to the level of humans defending words in the Bible as absolutely true. It is not the words that we need to prove true. It is the God who inspired the words that we need to prove true by living under His authority as sovereign Lord of life. Authority is not in the book so much as it is in the God who speaks to us in and through the book. We bear witness to the authority of Scripture by aligning our lives with its Spirit-inspired revelation. As people of one book, we participate in the world-shaping authority of God, which is clearly narrated in the book and thereby forms the Christian community.

Many will suggest that this is a liberal position, or a softening of the authority of Scripture. I disagree. To defend the words of Scripture is one step removed from living under that same Scripture in a vital relationship with God. The only text throughout the entire Bible that even comes close to suggesting that Scripture needs to be defended is the directive to young Timothy to guard the gospel. And these texts refer to a scandalous interpretation of the gospel of Jesus. Timothy is to tell the story right.

My fear is that we think we have done our part for God when we have defended placing the Ten Commandments on the courthouse wall or championed the right to teach the Bible in public schools. These are issues of importance, but they are not how we affirm the authority of God in our lives. Again, our concern is not to defend the authority of Scripture as a document, but to be transformed by bringing our lives under the authority of the God revealed in Scripture. A Baptist friend once asked me if Nazarenes believed in the inerrant, authoritative Word of God. I replied, "We go lots further than that. We actually believe that we should bring our lives into compliance with the God revealed in Scripture."

The apostle Paul was a man of Scripture. Trained in the law, steeped in the traditions of the law, faultless in keeping the law, he came to some remarkable conclusions about the written texts alone.

> If anyone else has reason to be confident in the flesh, I have more: circumcised on the eighth day, a member of the people of Israel, of the tribe of Benjamin, a Hebrew born of Hebrews; as to the law, a Pharisee; as to zeal, a persecutor of the church; as to righteousness under the law, blameless. Yet whatever gains I had, these I have come to regard as loss because of Christ. More than that, I regard everything as loss because of the surpassing value of knowing Christ Jesus my Lord. For his sake I have suffered the loss of all things, and I regard them as rubbish, in order that I may gain Christ and be found in him, not having a righteousness of my own that comes from the law, but one that comes through faith in Christ, the righteousness from God based on faith. I want to know Christ and the power of his resurrection and the sharing of his sufferings by becoming like him in his death, if somehow I may attain the resurrection from the dead. *(Phil. 3:4-11)*

Paul, as pre-Christian Saul, knew the letter of the law better than any of us, yet he did not perceive the authority of the One who became the Word and lived among us. It is possible to know the words and not know the Word. The written words, while authoritative as the Spirit-inspired revelation of God, are effective only as the revelation of the living Word.

Let me end this chapter with words from Paul that remind us that authority is not proved by the defense of words but by a transformed people.

> Are we beginning to commend ourselves again? Surely we do not need, as some do, letters of recommendation to you or from you, do we? You yourselves are our letter, writ-

ten on our hearts, to be known and read by all; and you show that you are a letter of Christ, prepared by us, written not with ink but with the Spirit of the living God, not on tablets of stone but on tablets of human hearts.

Such is the confidence that we have through Christ toward God. Not that we are competent of ourselves to claim anything as coming from us; our competence is from God, who has made us competent to be ministers of a new covenant, not of letter but of spirit; for the letter kills, but the Spirit gives life.

Now if the ministry of death, chiseled in letters on stone tablets, came in glory so that the people of Israel could not gaze at Moses' face because of the glory of his face, a glory now set aside, how much more will the ministry of the Spirit come in glory? For if there was glory in the ministry of condemnation, much more does the ministry of justification abound in glory! Indeed, what once had glory has lost its glory because of the greater glory; for if what was set aside came through glory, much more has the permanent come in glory!

Since, then, we have such a hope, we act with great boldness, not like Moses, who put a veil over his face to keep the people of Israel from gazing at the end of the glory that was being set aside. But their minds were hardened. Indeed, to this very day, when they hear the reading of the old covenant, that same veil is still there, since only in Christ is it set aside. Indeed, to this very day whenever Moses is read, a veil lies over their minds; but when one turns to the Lord, the veil is removed. Now the Lord is the Spirit, and where the Spirit of the Lord is, there is freedom. And all of us, with unveiled faces, seeing the glory of the Lord as though reflected in a mirror, are being transformed into the same image from one degree of glory to another; for this comes from the Lord, the Spirit. (2 Cor. 3)

3

THE GOD WHO TOLERATES NO RIVALS

Commandment 1

*Then God spoke all these words: I am the LORD your God,
who brought you out of the land of Egypt, out of the house of
slavery; you shall have no other gods before me.*
(Exod. 20:1-3)

I AM = imposes Action - I will
be always + Be for us

33

Do cell phone companies bug you as much as they do me? "Extend your contract—get one thousand bonus minutes!" "Switch and we'll send you a check for one hundred dollars! Get your whole family to switch, and we'll throw in text messaging! Get your town to switch, and we'll make you mayor!" New gimmicks. New deals. Companies compete viciously, all for your cell phone loyalty.

Freshmen at Trevecca Nazarene University know how this feels. The first week of school every club, cause, and church hits the campus. "Join us," "Pick me," "Sign here," "Free T-shirt," "Be cool." It's almost overwhelming for a person who's still wondering where Freshman Biology meets.

Loyalty of the people is a prize of high value. Our liberated friends in the wilderness were surrounded by gods. Behind them were the gods of Egypt, who for a while looked quite powerful and efficient. Then they met the God of the plagues. In front of them are the gods of the Canaanites. These gods are seductive. They offer good crops, rain, victory over the tribe next door, and plenty of children. Who doesn't want what's behind those doors? Gods, gods. Which to choose? Where to place your loyalty?

One of the interesting things about Christianity is that our God does not stand in a line of world religions like club rush day and say, "Pick me; please pick me!" In the words of Jesus, "You did not choose me, but I chose you" (John 15:16). We do not find God, God finds us. Long before we were freshmen in the search for life's meaning, the God and Father of our Lord Jesus Christ had already created the world in love, offered us His covenant, demonstrated His love in the flesh-and-blood Jesus, and atoned for our sins.

The first commandment is matter-of-fact. "I am your God, and there will be no other gods." He actually said, "No other gods before my face." When God looks at us, He wants to see our face, not the face of another who has captured our loyalty. But in today's world, with the Egyptian and Canaanite gods out of the picture, what gods might threaten such loyalty? Profit-loss columns, Wii, the new Lexus, our favorite reality show, workaholism, perfectionism, NASCAR, exercise, romance novels, sports, food, the latest movie, the new diet, politics, shopping, prescription drugs, playing video games, the girl, the boy, shopping, shoes, hair, stuff, money. Most anything or anyone can be turned into a god if you stare at it long enough and eventually bow to it.

But Bob Dylan was right. "You gotta serve somebody," and God wants exclusive rights. Some have questioned such a God. Why does God need our undivided attention and unquestioned loyalty? Is He insecure? Demanding? Paranoid? What kind of a weak God is this?

Oprah Winfrey raised the question on national TV. It has made the circuit of Christian cultural watchdogs. Her words were like a piece of raw meat tossed into a lions' den. She said, "I was raised a Baptist and we were too hung up on traditional ways. I was sitting in church and heard that God is a jealous God. I asked 'Why?' Come on—let's get over it!"[1] She went on to question why God might be jealous of her. Many took this to mean that she viewed God as jealous in a coveting sort of way—that God was miffed because she was getting all the attention. I don't think this is what she meant. I think she was asking a question that many people ask—why is God so demanding? For Oprah, this question led to her impatience with rules, belief systems, and doctrines. Sadly, the gift of God—law as a picture of how the redeemed live—was misunderstood. And Oprah could have found a very good dance partner in the Ten Commandments.

Imagine yourself as a craftsperson. You are expecting your first child. You carefully select a pattern and plan for a cradle. You go to the lumberyard and choose the finest, straightest, most beautiful cherry boards available. You spend hours in your woodwork shop, never once looking at a clock. Time passes as you are caught up in the loving act of creation. You measure twice before cutting once. You refuse to make allowances for any quarter-of-an-inch mistake. You plane and cut and groove and assemble and sand. In selecting a stain, you test several candidates on scrap wood before settling for the right one—a stain that allows the natural grain to emerge without erasing the beauty already in the wood. You apply the stain with circular hand movements, rubbing it deep into the wood. You wipe the residue carefully. You seal and sand, seal and sand, until the triple-coated surface is smooth as the bottom of the baby to be born. Your masterpiece is complete, waiting for the birth of the child you have loved before his or her creation. Imagine then, that one day, another craftsperson comes into your workshop, sees the cradle, and suggests that this would be a good storage bin for tools. It is sturdy, has plenty of room, and could hold several hand tools. This craftsperson claims the cradle for this purpose. You are incensed and guard your creation jealously. You know why the cradle was created and who it was created for. You refuse to allow that which was made for one purpose to be used for a less dignified purpose.

This is a jealousy rooted in love. This jealousy does not rise from a paranoid tyrant, but from a loving creator. It is on behalf of the loved, not the lover. It is a saving attitude and action. It makes claims on behalf of those who have no clue what other gods intend to do with them.

Deep in our heart of hearts, we all want to be loved like that. The slaves of Egypt did. The exiles of Babylon did. They wanted a God who would bring them to completion as creatures. They wanted a God who desired for them communities of justice, mercy, and grace. They wanted a God who was not capricious, not moody, and not fickle. They wanted a God who had no need to be elaborately placated. But how would they know such a God? They would experience this God in day-to-day life. This God would be the source of the experience of their fathers—Abraham, Isaac, Jacob, and Joseph. This God would make demands through covenant, offer blessing to generations, and provide a place/land for life to happen.

There are plenty of cell phone companies that promise you the moon, plenty of clubs to join, and plenty of causes to sign up for. Choose them, and they will reward you. Shun them, and they will go on to the next prospective pawn. But there is only one God who will not sleep until you know that you have been fearfully and wonderfully knit together under divine optimism, given a world of provision for life, and claimed by blood shed on your behalf in a decisive moment of history. This God will not rest until you know that you are made in His image and likeness. This God claims you as a child. This God moves heaven and earth to liberate you from all the imposters, tyrants, and seducers. This God knows that the gods can only enslave and kill. This God gives life, abundantly. That's why this God tolerates no rivals.

To be loved like this is a gift.

HOLY TERROR

Commandment 2

*You shall not make for yourself an idol, whether in the form of anything that is in heaven above, or that is on the earth beneath, or that is in the water under the earth. You shall not bow down to them or worship them; for I the L*ORD *your God am a jealous God, punishing children for the iniquity of parents, to the third and the fourth generation of those who reject me, but showing steadfast love to the thousandth generation of those who love me and keep my commandments.*
(Exod. 20:4-6)

For some reason, after reading this commandment, the words that linger with us are "but showing steadfast love to the thousandth generation of those who love me and keep my commandments" (v. 6). These words lift an inch off the page and beg our attention. All the other words, words like "jealous God, punishing children . . . to the third and the fourth generation," are barely remembered once we finish reading.

While we wish to ignore these parts of Scripture, we cannot. The Bible is as full of holy terror as it is tender love. Ask our wilderness friends in Exodus. Having experienced the death of every firstborn in Egypt, they took God at His word. Having seen the God of fire and thunder on Mount Sinai, the people had no doubt about God's capacity to vent. So the Bible speaks of both love and terror. But in our new age of terrorism, making God out as a terrorist is not advantageous for the seeker-sensitive church working hard not to offend or for the emergent church trying so hard to recapture a generation grown up on Columbine, 9-11, Iraq, and Virginia Tech. These texts are not good PR for God.

And how do parents explain to their children a God who asks Abraham to slaughter and roast his only son in one Testament, and then sends His own only Son to a cruel crucifixion in the other Testament? And how does a world of individualism find any justice in sin being punished three and four generations later? Few of us wish to be God's spokesperson answering for these actions. This law we dare not dance with. It is a dreadful thing to fall into the hands of a living God.

One of the ways we try to deal with these texts of terror is to suggest that those who obey God are "terror-exempt."[2] The commandment would seem to suggest that the obedient get steadfast love for a thousand generations and the disobedient get living hell for three or four generations. This serves us well when we wish to threaten people into righteous living. But when we widen the scope of the biblical narrative, "Job stands on one side of the pulpit shaking his head and Jesus on the other, both of them confirming our fear that righteousness does nothing to dissuade God from trying the faithful by fire and by ice."[3] Our book has frightening things in it, and we cannot explain them away—which also means that our God is radically different and cannot be predicted or understood by the creatures He creates. We stand before Him in awe.

When she was three years old, I took my granddaughter to Chuck E. Cheese. You know, "Where a kid can be a kid." It's an indoor carnival of games, entertainment, music, and not-so-good pizza. Chuck is a costumed seven-foot mouse who prowls the place high-fiving kids and having fun. But when Anna Ryan, age three, saw him, she retreated in terror and latched herself to my leg with a death grip. No explanation could shake her loose. "He's just a nice man in a suit. It's not real, just a costume. See, all the other children are playing with him." She had no categories for a seven-foot mouse that walked among mere babes, and nothing I did or said could change her mind that something just didn't seem right about that mouse.

To be encountered by a God of punitive jealousy causes us to clutch our fixed ideas about who God is and how God operates. We prefer a settled God, predictable in every way, not One who seems too big as He prowls among weaklings with the power to crush. Maybe the terror texts do their work when they unsettle us. Maybe we are meant to be aware that we are in the presence of One for whom there are no categories of likeness. Maybe we are supposed to realize that our God is not a stranger to judgment, violence, terror, and death. Maybe we are supposed to think about the long-term effects of our sin. Maybe the texts still drive us toward the God whose mystery is magnetic.

These days Anna Ryan likes Chuck E. Cheese. She has gotten used to him, almost. I asked her the other day about going on a date to Chuck's place. She thought for a minute and said, "OK." Her hesitancy caused me to ask her what she thought about the mouse. Her reply was sacred. "I'm still just a little bit scared." Not a bad posture before the God of terrors.

Barbara Brown Taylor tells the story of a loggerhead turtle in her excellent article "Preaching the Terrors." The turtle had made its way from the ocean to the beach to lay her eggs in a sand nest. After watching for a while, Barbara left, so as not to disturb the turtle. The next day, she noticed that the tracks of the turtle led, not toward the ocean, but into the blistering dunes. As she followed the tracks, she found the turtle exhausted and nearly baked. Finding a park ranger with a jeep, she watched him set out to rescue the turtle. She writes:

> As I watched in horror, he flipped her over on her back, wrapped tire chains around her front legs, and hooked the chains to the trailer hitch on his jeep. Then he took off, yanking her body forward so fast that her open mouth filled with sand and then disappeared underneath her as her neck bent so far I feared it would break.
>
> The ranger hauled her over the dunes and down onto the beach; I followed the path that the prow of her shell cut in the sand. At ocean's edge, he unhooked her and turned her right side up again. She lay motionless in the surf as the water lapped at her body, washing the sand from her eyes and making her skin shine again.
>
> Then a particularly large wave broke over her, and she lifted her head slightly, moving her back legs as she did. As I watched, she revived. Every fresh wave brought her life back to her until one of them made her light enough to find a foothold and push off, back into the water that was her home.
>
> Watching her swim slowly away and remembering her nightmare ride through the dunes, I noted that it is sometimes hard to tell whether you are being killed or saved by the hands that turn your life upside down.[4]

LAUGHING AT IDOLS

Commandment 2, Continued

You shall not make for yourself an idol, whether in the form of anything that is in heaven above, or that is on the earth beneath, or that is in the water under the earth. You shall not bow down to them or worship them; for I the LORD your God am a jealous God, punishing children for the iniquity of parents, to the third and the fourth generation of those who reject me, but showing steadfast love to the thousandth generation of those who love me and keep my commandments.
(Exod. 20:4-6)

Passionately zealous not
jealous

Sat. night - Cancer
Karen & Greg

During Amy's high school years, she was in a play. The setting of the play was a unique high school. In this town, the school board had met and decided to send all the bad kids to one high school. You had bullies and boozers, gangs and slackers, hotheads and foulmouths. The only qualification for being in this school was getting kicked out of the other schools in town. As the play unfolds, some good kids are mistakenly assigned to this high school and are faced with the challenge of surviving. Thus the title of the play, *Help, I'm Trapped in a High School.*

The plotline of this play could have easily come from the Old Testament. The school would be named Exile High. The main characters—the Jews—had grown up in Jerusalem under the shadow of Temple, priest, messianic king, divine law, sacrifice, and blessing. Now, they woke up every morning in a strange land where the language was different, the culture crude, and the food odd. They were trapped in a Babylonian exile. They didn't belong here. There must have been some mistake in the divine assignment office. Like Dorothy in Oz, there was nothing they wanted more than to go home.

But Babylon has other ideas for them. It was the business of Babylon to conquer people, resettle them in a strange place, erase their religious and cultural memory, and turn them slowly into good citizens of the empire. Babylon would build its kingdom on re-formed Jews. And Babylon was relentless. Its language was dominant, its economic rewards were tangible, and its gods were celebrated.

Bel and Nebo were hoisted onto the backs of animals and paraded from Babylon to Borsippa. People bowed and cheered and offered elaborate sacrifice to the gods who had given them the victory over the Jews and all the other peon peoples being re-formed.

Surrounded by overwhelming power, who could resist? For a while the Jews held their own, remembered their ways, spoke their language, and told their stories. But the day-by-day pounding of a pagan culture wore them down. Why not speak the language? Why not make a buck or two? Why not go to the parade of the gods and enjoy a little merriment in this drab world? What's the harm?

We can understand their position. As the baptized people of God, we are trapped in a culture that runs opposite to the ways of our God. Its pounding is relentless. Its pressure is persistent. The gods have different names. Instead of Bel and Nebo, we have financial security, military superiority, political victory, social acceptance, physical appearance, business dominance, sexual expression. We hoist these gods on the backs of technology, marketing, and entertainment and parade them from New York to L.A. We cheer and bow and sacrifice ourselves to these idols. Those blessed by the gods become our heroes and idols. And sadly, we baptized folk drool after them along with the born and bred pagans of the land. We want to be millionaires. We want to be viewed as hot and sexy. We want bombs that can blast our enemies to bits. We want our party to win. We want popularity with the masses. We want our fifteen minutes of fame. We want to climb to the top of the success ladder and enjoy the view.

Babylon is seductive.

It seems to me that we have three options:

1. We can be assimilated. Capitulate, surrender, give up. Join the parade. Throw in the towel and go with the flow. After all, this Jesus way is too odd, too demanding, too tough. Resistance is futile. Why fight it?

2. We can despair. We can nurse our feelings of abandonment and helplessness. We can live nostalgically, remembering the good old days of our Jerusalem past. If we can get enough despairing people together, we can build a fortress to protect our memories. Grousing about how things used to be is a good pastime for nonengaged nostalgia.

3. We can laugh at the idols. This is the choice of the Babylonian exile writer in Isa. 46.

Bel bows down, Nebo stoops,
    their idols are on beasts and cattle;
these things you carry are loaded
    as burdens on weary animals.
They stoop, they bow down together;
    they cannot save the burden,
    but themselves go into captivity.

Listen to me, O house of Jacob,
    all the remnant of the house of Israel,
who have been borne by me from your birth,
    carried from the womb;
even to your old age I am he,
    even when you turn gray I will carry you.
I have made, and I will bear;
    I will carry and will save.

To whom will you liken me and make me equal,
    and compare me, as though we were alike?
Those who lavish gold from the purse,
    and weigh out silver in the scales—
they hire a goldsmith, who makes it into a god;
    then they fall down and worship!
They lift it to their shoulders, they carry it,
    they set it in its place, and it stands there;
    it cannot move from its place.
If one cries out to it, it does not answer
    or save anyone from trouble.

Remember this and consider,
    recall it to mind, you transgressors,
    remember the former things of old;
for I am God, and there is no other;
    I am God, and there is no one like me,

declaring the end from the beginning
   and from ancient times things not yet done,
saying, "My purpose shall stand,
   and I will fulfill my intention,"
calling a bird of prey from the east,
   the man for my purpose from a far country.
I have spoken, and I will bring it to pass;
   I have planned, and I will do it.

Listen to me, you stubborn of heart,
   you who are far from deliverance:
I bring near my deliverance, it is not far off,
   and my salvation will not tarry;
I will put salvation in Zion,
   for Israel my glory.

The dominant gods of Babylon have to be helped by humans. Beasts of burden carry them. They cannot move on their own. Only with human help do they get around. They are mute. They are the product of goldsmiths and craftsmen. But, oh, the fuss made over them! Like the chubby little man behind the Oz curtain (otherwise known as the Wizard of Oz), there is little substance to the impressive display of power. It's mostly special effects.

I don't know about you, but I'll take option No. 3. We refuse to take these gods seriously, because they have no power to get us home. We refuse to be assimilated by them or sacrifice to them, because they are not living gods. They are a laughingstock. Laughter is a rebellious act that defies the way the dying world operates. It is subversive, costly, liberating, and courageous.

So we laugh in a liberating, courageous, in-your-face way
      at the gods of advertising who tell us that our happiness
         is packaged as a product
      at the gods of porn who suggest that other humans are
         fuel for our lust

    at the gods of fashion who dictate our clothing brands
        and budget

    at the gods of consumption and overdevelopment who
        strip the earth bare and leave nothing for the next
        generation

    at the gods of alcohol who numb our brains, enslave our
        friends, and kill our families

    at the gods of sexual expression who champion one-
        night stands over lifelong bonds

    at the gods of politics who promise what cannot be de-
        livered in exchange for the power to rule

    at the gods of prestige and greed who spend on show
        what the poor need for bread

    at the gods of popular approval who read opinion polls
        to find out where they stand

    at the gods of sports who consume our time and en-
        throne winning above all else

    at the gods of fame who contest for being a survivor on
        an island, an idol in America, or a biggest loser

The world would give anything to be blessed by these gods. And we have the option of being assimilated and joining the parade of these gods. Or we can waste our lives in despair. But we choose to laugh because our God is infinitely superior.

    Our God does not need to be carried. Our God carries us.

    Our God is not created. Our God creates.

    Our God is not made with human hands. Our God makes
    human hands.

    Our God does not need to be protected by humans. Our God
    saves.

The Ten Commandments find fertile ground when placed in the context of the Babylonian exile.

    You shall not make for yourself an idol, whether in the form of anything that is in heaven above, or that is on the earth beneath, or that is in the water under the earth. You shall not bow down to them or worship them; for I the LORD your God am a jealous God, punishing children for the iniquity of parents, to the third and the fourth generation of those who reject me, but showing steadfast love to the thousandth generation of those who love me and keep my commandments. *(Exod. 20:4-6)*

They were in Babylon because of the encroaching sins of their fathers and their disobedience in the land God had given them. Their God had not forgotten them. He could bring them home from Babylon just as He brought them home from Egypt. Bel could not deliver. Nebo could not carry them. Their hope rested in the God who brought them out of the house of slavery.

Ours does too. Refuse to be assimilated. Don't despair. Laugh at the gods.

Passionately Zealous
Not
Jealous

6

PLAGIARIZING THE NAME OF GOD

Commandment 3

You shall not make wrongful use of the name of the LORD your God,
for the LORD will not acquit anyone who misuses his name.

(Exod. 20:7)

It costs $1 million to use the name. Krispy Kreme is a doughnut franchise born in heaven. If you've ever tasted one of these southern delicacies, you'll agree. If you "get 'em while they're hot," they literally melt in your mouth. The franchise price tag is $1 million.

But compared to "Disney," "Krispy Kreme" is pocket change. Last time I checked, Disney's name is worth $15 million. You get the rights to the name with all the legal requirements attached. There are places you can and can't use the name. Things you can and can't do with it. If you pilfer, slander, or misuse the name, you will meet the well-heeled lawyers whose job it is to protect the use of the Disney name.

That's a lot of money and a lot of rules when it comes to something as simple as the use of a name—wouldn't you say? "You shall not make wrongful use of the name of the LORD your God, for the LORD will not acquit anyone who misuses his name" (Exod. 20:7). The Kings James Version tells us to "not take the name of the LORD . . . in vain." Eugene Peterson in *The Message* paraphrases it, "No using the name of GOD, your God, in curses or silly banter; GOD won't put up with the irreverent use of his name."

Let's see if we can dance with this law. Our first instinct is that this commandment forbids cussing. Especially the kind of cussing that includes words like *God* and *Jesus Christ* and *holy* and *Mother of God* and . . . well, you get the point. In our culture, using God's name in a curse or as a curse certainly fits the category of misuse or irreverence. But this isn't the primary meaning of the command.

One of the mistakes we make in reading the Bible is to see a text only through the lens of our current culture. When we do this, we limit ourselves to discovering less than what is actually there for us. While the Scriptures can certainly be applied forward in time, they find a better home among us when we begin with their written context. Cussing wasn't that big of a problem in Moses' day. I doubt there were a bunch of foulmouthed Jews running around in the wilderness (or in Babylon) turning the air blue with their profanity. The idea that they'd be swearing a blue streak about the God who liberated them from slavery is preposterous.

The issue is the use of God's name in keeping with God's character and action.

This is why Krispy Kreme and Disney are so protective of their names. The name stands for the essence of who they are and what they do. They do not wish their name cheapened by the misuse of it. Jimmy Bob's doughnuts may be good, but he can't take his granny's recipe and affix the name Krispy Kreme to the front window of his gas station. It just isn't Krispy Kreme.

Moses wanted to know the name of the voice that spoke from the bush that burned but didn't burn up. At that time, knowing the name of a god meant being able to use the power of that god in ways that would come in handy. It's why Moses wanted to be armed with the answer to Pharaoh's anticipated question, "And just what God is it who demands that I let these people go?" Moses was given two names—"the God of your father, the God of Abraham, the God of Isaac, and the God of Jacob" (Exod. 3:6). Quite a long name, but rich in rooted history and significantly developed in character. The other name was less lengthy, but more mysterious: "I AM WHO I AM" (v. 14).

But Moses never used either. Before Pharaoh, he referred to God as Yahweh, or the LORD. He also called Him the God of the Hebrews. It didn't work. Pharaoh wasn't impressed by the name, and he raised the brick quota. He was sure his gods were equal to or greater than this God of riffraff people. So God spoke again to Moses:

> Then the LORD said to Moses, "Now you shall see what I will do to Pharaoh: Indeed, by a mighty hand he will let them go; by a mighty hand he will drive them out of his land." God also spoke to Moses and said to him: "I am the

LORD. I appeared to Abraham, Isaac, and Jacob as God Almighty, but by my name 'The LORD' [Yahweh] I did not make myself known to them. I also established my covenant with them, to give them the land of Canaan, the land in which they resided as aliens. I have also heard the groaning of the Israelites whom the Egyptians are holding as slaves, and I have remembered my covenant. Say therefore to the Israelites, 'I am the LORD, and I will free you from the burdens of the Egyptians and deliver you from slavery to them. I will redeem you with an outstretched arm and with mighty acts of judgment. I will take you as my people, and I will be your God. You shall know that I am the LORD your God, who has freed you from the burdens of the Egyptians. I will bring you into the land that I swore to give to Abraham, Isaac, and Jacob; I will give it to you for a possession. I am the LORD.'" Moses told this to the Israelites; but they would not listen to Moses, because of their broken spirit and their cruel slavery.

Then the LORD spoke to Moses, "Go and tell Pharaoh king of Egypt to let the Israelites go out of his land." But Moses spoke to the LORD, "The Israelites have not listened to me; how then shall Pharaoh listen to me, poor speaker that I am?" Thus the LORD spoke to Moses and Aaron, and gave them orders regarding the Israelites and Pharaoh king of Egypt, charging them to free the Israelites from the land of Egypt. *(Exod. 6:1-13)*

The power of God is not in the name of God but in the character of the God who is being called upon in the mention of the name. Different from other ancient gods, this name is not magic, but history. God's saving activity does not occur because some sly leader has gotten hold of the magic words/names, but because God is at work in history. God is redeeming His people and making all things new. Pharaoh did not bow to this God because he feared the name, but because this God acted in ways that humbled him and brought his nation to its knees. The name

simply evoked the presence of a God who could not be manip-
ulated for human purposes and was stubbornly at work doing
what He willed. It was not the name that liberated Israel but the
activity of the God called Yahweh, the God of the Hebrews, the
God of Abraham and Isaac and Jacob, the God we call the God
and Father of our Lord Jesus Christ, or Trinity for short.

In the Lord's Prayer, Jesus teaches us to pray "hallowed be
your name" (Matt. 6:9). The name of God is to be reverenced
and treated as holy. We use it only where God is being named
as active in the world. The warning in the Sermon on the Mount
is stern: "Not everyone who says to me, 'Lord, Lord,' will enter
the kingdom of heaven, but only the one who does the will of
my Father in heaven. On that day many will say to me, 'Lord,
Lord, did we not prophesy in your name, and cast out demons in
your name, and do many deeds of power in your name?' Then
I will declare to them, 'I never knew you; go away from me, you
evildoers'" (7:21-23).

So God's name is not to be taken lightly. You don't casually
stick this name on your idea, product, or words. You had better
be sure that you are actually doing what God is doing before you
affix His name to your agenda. To plagiarize the name of God
is to use His name for what He is not doing. Many things done
"in the name of God" are not the doings of God. A history of
religious war, prejudice, sexual abuse, and scandal testify to this.
And you better believe that God is more insistent than Krispy
Kreme or Disney about not using His name in a way that reflects
wrongly on His character or associates Him with what He is not
doing.

To pray that God's name be hallowed in us may be one of
the deepest prayers for sanctification in the Bible. We are asking
to be made like God in action and character so that His name,
attached to our words and deeds, will be reverenced as a true
reflection of who He is.

SHA-

7
THE PINOCCHIO EFFECT

Commandment 3, Continued

You shall not make wrongful use of the name of the LORD your God,
for the LORD will not acquit anyone who misuses his name.
(Exod. 20:7)

Bill trashed the name of God with casual regularity. GD to him was normal language. His parents swore, his aunts and uncles swore, his school buddies swore. It wasn't that anybody set out to abuse the name of God; it was just their cultural language. It came with the territory.

In all honesty, Bill was ignorant about God's command. He meant nothing by it—and no one had ever said a word to him about his profanity. Bill was uninformed about the seriousness of using God's name.

Then Bill met a genuine, authentic, honest believer whose life was consistent, a new friend deeply devoted to God. Bill liked hanging around with this guy and soon began to experience God's accepting love through him. He was under conviction because the very God he cursed actually cared about him. But Bill's resistance ran deep, and he responded to God's gentle prodding by pushing back. He intentionally started offending his new Christian friend, notching up the profanity, looking for the opportunity to embarrass him.

One day, the friend confronted Bill: "Did you know that 'd—n' is not God's last name? You probably have no idea what it does to me when you trash God's name like that. The God I serve isn't into d—ning, He's into blessing. He has made my life meaningful in every way."

Bill became even more arrogant. His profanity was no longer casual; it was intentional. Cursing became Bill's way of raising his fist in the face of God. It was his way of saying, "I'm in charge here. I'm not buying this religion bit. I will not bow to You."

But something began to happen to Bill. Each time he cursed the name of God, he became aware of the presence of the God he cursed. He realized that he was actually addressing God, provoking a response of presence. And Bill was softened by the exchange. As he recognized the emptiness of his life compared to that of his friend, he began to crumble. One day, he sat in his car leaning over the steering wheel, contemplating his life. And he prayed. "God, it's me—the tough guy with the foul mouth. I've trashed Your name a million times. I've dared You to do something about it. But You have done nothing to d—n me back. You just keep making me aware of You. Apparently, I matter to You. I want to know You as more than a curse word. Forgive me." And God did. And Bill believed.

As a new Christian, Bill started working on his language, but the tongue is a tough tiger to tame. Profanity had become a natural part of his response mechanism, and it would take awhile to dislodge the speech patterns. Habits die hard.

One day when Bill was in his small-group meeting, the guys were reading James 3:7: "Every species of beast and bird, of reptile and sea creature, can be tamed and has been tamed by the human species, but no one can tame the tongue—a restless evil, full of deadly poison." Bill agreed with James. But he was up to the challenge of taming the tongue. He committed to an accountability process with his group. They would ask him each week if he had spoken profanity of any kind, and he would give an honest answer. He did well—except for the time he backed his rental car into another vehicle and the time he was with some old high school buddies and the time he was telling his small group about his first witnessing experience and how it felt: "D—n good." They forgave him with laughter for the last one.

Bill stayed at it, and the Spirit of God saturated his heart and slowly replaced cursing with blessing. Bill's use of God's name became purposeful, intentional, and uplifting as he shared with family and friends how God had blessed his life. And now, the mere mention of God's name made Bill aware of God's power and presence. He could hardly believe the person he used to be.

As Bill bought into Christianity, he started tasting all its flavors. It wasn't long until he met the television evangelists. Their "name it and claim it" simplicity caught his attention. In Jesus' name people were healed, riches were promised, and miracles offered. Preachers, teachers, and visiting celebrities spoke so naturally of having talked with God that very day and having been told by God that 167 people were going to send $500 to the broadcast. One man was told by God that the Second Coming would happen in January. Another woman said that God had instructed her to leave her husband and children so she could devote herself more fully to the ministry. It seemed that if God's name was attached to it, nothing was questioned. And Bill was hooked. He wanted in on this kind of power. It was like having a magic lantern, a genie in a bottle, God in a box. Rub the lantern, summon the genie, crank the handle, and presto—it happened. Out comes God with His name affixed to your command or wish.

Bill learned the art quickly. To his dad: "God told me to buy this car and to ask you for the down payment." To an eligible young woman: "God told me to ask you out." To his preacher: "God told me that your sermons are not tough enough on sin." It was like having blank checks, signed by God. So Bill cashed them. To the woman dying with cancer: "God says if you have enough faith, you'll be healed." To a friend breaking off an engagement because of signals of abuse: "God told me if you'll stay in the relationship, you will lead him to Christ." To a friend opening a new business: "God told me your business will not succeed in this location."

Bill used God's name with casual regularity to endorse his own will. He labeled his thoughts and leanings and leadings with the divine logo. And God was grieved. Bill was using the franchise name without authorization. So God decided to deal with Bill.

Each time Bill misused God's name, God grew his ears by one-fourth of an inch. It was a Pinocchio effect, except this time it was the ears instead of the nose. Every time Bill signed a blank check with God's name on it, his ears grew. The first one-fourth, half, and three-fourths of an inch didn't get his attention. He had noticed that his baseball cap was sitting a little higher on his head, but nothing more. A couple of days later, someone remarked that he resembled Ross Perot. Then a few days after that, a four-year-old pointed and said, "Look, Mom, Dumbo the Elephant!"

By this time his ears were even with the top of his head and the bottom of his jaw. And Bill was scouring the yellow pages for a plastic surgeon. He kept trying to figure out what was going on. He carried a retractable Craftsman measuring tape with him to figure out when his ears were sprouting.

Finally, he figured out the cause-and-effect mechanics. It happened when he was chastising his mother for not submitting to the head of the house as the Bible says, noting that God had told him that she should worship her husband. That one added a whole inch and a half!

Every time Bill spoke for God when God hadn't spoken, every time he used God's name to enforce his will, every time he forged his opinion with God's signature, his ears grew. Bill had perfected the art of using God, and in the process God's presence had disappeared.

It is easier to place God at our disposal than to place ourselves at God's disposal. It is easier to call for the genie, than to serve the Master.

Bill's crumbling humility and repentance reminded him of the day he bowed over the steering wheel and asked God to forgive him for his foul mouth. That night he wrote these words in his journal: "The worst blasphemy is not profanity, but lip service—to speak God's name, without God's backing, to talk as if God does not hear and is not present to defend His name."

The prayer says it well: "Our Father in heaven, hallowed be your name."

Reverence

SABBATH

Commandment 4

Remember the sabbath day, and keep it holy. Six days you shall labor and do all your work. But the seventh day is a sabbath to the LORD your God; you shall not do any work—you, your son or your daughter, your male or female slave, your livestock, or the alien resident in your towns. For in six days the LORD made heaven and earth, the sea, and all that is in them, but rested the seventh day; therefore the LORD blessed the sabbath day and consecrated it.

(Exod 20:8-11)

Everybody I know is tired. You are tired. I am tired. Your work wears on you. Your expenditure of energy in people, places, and things drains you. Your spirit is fatigued. You shoulder major responsibility. You make life-altering decisions. You hire and fire. You give counsel. You care for an elderly person. You keep an eye on a feeble neighbor. You bake a casserole for the funeral of a friend. You listen to complaining people. You hammer nails. You chase a toddler all day long and then wake up three times a night to coax him back to sleep.

In addition to the work, you battle the monotony of doing the same things repeatedly. Laundry breeds in the closet. School homework is eternal. Customers keep showing up. Things break and require fixing, again. Grass grows. Snow has to be shoveled. Reports are due by the end of the week. Little ones hit the floor feet and mouths running. Paperwork stacks up. Planes line up on the runway. Your inbox, mailbox, and voicemail are full. Bills stack up. Groceries disappear. Gas tanks plummet toward empty.

We've done these things all our lives, every week, most days. And we grow tired of the rat race.

May I tell you one of my favorite stories?

Once upon a time the Creator created creation. As the story is told in Gen. 1, we notice a literary flow. It's hard to see unless you magnify the pattern words. Observe the pattern:

> In the beginning when God created the heavens and the earth, the earth was a formless void and darkness covered the face of the deep, while a wind from God swept over the face of the waters. Then God said, "Let there be light"; and there was light. And God saw that the light was good; and God separated the light from the darkness. God called the light Day, and the darkness he called Night. And there was evening and there was morning, the first day.
>
> And God said, "Let there be a dome in the midst of the waters, and let it separate the waters from the waters." So

God made the dome and separated the waters that were under the dome from the waters that were above the dome. And it was so. God called the dome Sky. And there was evening and there was morning, the second day.

And God said, "Let the waters under the sky be gathered together into one place, and let the dry land appear." And it was so. God called the dry land Earth, and the waters that were gathered together he called Seas. And God saw that it was good. Then God said, "Let the earth put forth vegetation: plants yielding seed, and fruit trees of every kind on earth that bear fruit with the seed in it." And it was so. The earth brought forth vegetation: plants yielding seed of every kind, and trees of every kind bearing fruit with the seed in it. And God saw that it was good. And there was evening and there was morning, the third day.

And God said, "Let there be lights in the dome of the sky to separate the day from the night; and let them be for signs and for seasons and for days and years, and let them be lights in the dome of the sky to give light upon the earth." And it was so. God made the two great lights—the greater light to rule the day and the lesser light to rule the night—and the stars. God set them in the dome of the sky to give light upon the earth, to rule over the day and over the night, and to separate the light from the darkness. And God saw that it was good. And there was evening and there was morning, the fourth day.

And God said, "Let the waters bring forth swarms of living creatures, and let birds fly above the earth across the dome of the sky." So God created the great sea monsters and every living creature that moves, of every kind, with which the waters swarm, and every winged bird of every kind. And God saw that it was good. God blessed them, saying, "Be fruitful and multiply and fill the waters in the seas, and let birds multiply on the earth." And there was evening and there was morning, the fifth day.

And God said, "Let the earth bring forth living creatures of every kind: cattle and creeping things and wild animals of the earth of every kind." And it was so. God made the wild animals of the earth of every kind, and the cattle of every kind, and everything that creeps upon the ground of every kind. And God saw that it was good.

Then God said, "Let us make humankind in our image, according to our likeness; and let them have dominion over the fish of the sea, and over the birds of the air, and over the cattle, and over all the wild animals of the earth, and over every creeping thing that creeps upon the earth."

So God created humankind in his image, in the image of God he created them; male and female he created them. God blessed them, and God said to them, "Be fruitful and multiply, and fill the earth and subdue it; and have dominion over the fish of the sea and over the birds of the air and over every living thing that moves upon the earth." God said, "See, I have given you every plant yielding seed that is upon the face of all the earth, and every tree with seed in its fruit; you shall have them for food. And to every beast of the earth, and to every bird of the air, and to everything that creeps on the earth, everything that has the breath of life, I have given every green plant for food." And it was so. God saw everything that he had made, and indeed, it was very good. And there was evening and there was morning, the sixth day. *(Gen. 1)*

Evening/morning, evening/morning. Each new day begins with night. When we go to sleep, God begins the new day. We begin each day resting. While we're sawing logs, God is recalibrating His creation. The moon marks the seasons. The waves clean the shores. The lion stalks its prey. Earthworms aerate the land. Proteins repair our damaged muscles. Enzymes digest our food. Night cools the earth. Dew refreshes the ground. We wake up in a universe humming with the creative activity of God.

This cycle tells us that the world does not hinge on our work. We make our contribution late in the day. God was putting the finishing touches on creation when we were hired on day six. For all our industriousness and ingenuity, our acquisitiveness and acquiring, our competing and completing, the world does not hinge on what we do. Take us out of the picture and life goes on.

Our fit in this evening/morning pattern is sleep/labor, sleep/labor. Interestingly, there is no biblical command to sleep. It's a pattern we can't ignore without crashing. Our bodies demand sleep. The creation story establishes a healthy pattern—evening/morning, sleep/labor.

But there's another pattern in the story:

Thus the heavens and the earth were finished, and all their multitude. And on the seventh day God finished the work that he had done, and he rested on the seventh day from all the work that he had done. So God blessed the seventh day and hallowed it, because on it God rested from all the work that he had done in creation. *(Gen. 2:1-3)*

After creating, God rested. God practiced Sabbath. The word *Sabbath* means stop, quit, cease and desist, rest. God stopped doing what he had been doing for six days. A new rhythm began. Six days of labor, one day of rest: 6/1, 6/1, 6/1, 6/1.

Fast-forward in time. We find ourselves in Egypt, slaves in a brick-making factory. We have a slave-driving boss. We submitted a request for a religious holiday out in the wilderness park, but the boss got ticked and figured we had too much time on our hands. Our brick quota has just been raised again. We are tired. We do the same monotonous things every day. We've been working ten hours a day, seven days a week, fifty-two weeks a year, for four hundred years. How's that for a rhythm?

Here comes God liberating us from Pharaoh's grind and preparing us for a new career as entrepreneurs in Canaan. We stand at the foot of a smoking mountain to hear the new commands. And God says:

> Remember the sabbath day, and keep it holy. Six days you shall labor and do all your work. But the seventh day is a sabbath to the LORD your God; you shall not do any work—you, your son or your daughter, your male or female slave, your livestock, or the alien resident in your towns. For in six days the LORD made heaven and earth, the sea, and all that is in them, but rested the seventh day; therefore the LORD blessed the sabbath day and consecrated it. *(Exod. 20:8-11)*

For the life of me, I cannot imagine any liberated slave saying, "What! No way! If I want to work seven days a week, who are you to tell me I can't? No one has the right to make me stop working!" They would have called that slave crazy. Today we call the same person a workhorse, the backbone of the company, the guts of the organization, an iron man (or woman). We give that person awards and make him or her the poster child of productivity.

And there are also those people who work six days for pay, then become nonstop workers at other quests on the seventh day—white knuckling a golf club and getting more stressed with each hole, attacking the lawn with veins bulging, cleaning the house with the vengeance of germ warfare. They are restless, driven, anxious, charging, doing-doing-doing. And God speaks a gift from the holy mountain: "Stop!"

Are we listening?

A little later in the Exodus story, God says:

> You shall keep the sabbath, because it is holy for you; everyone who profanes it shall be put to death; whoever does any work on it shall be cut off from among the people. Six days shall work be done, but the seventh day is a sabbath of solemn rest, holy to the LORD; whoever does any work on the sabbath day shall be put to death. Therefore the Israelites shall keep the sabbath, observing the sabbath throughout their generations, as a perpetual covenant. It is a sign forever

between me and the people of Israel that in six days the LORD made heaven and earth, and on the seventh day he rested, and was refreshed. *(Exod. 31:14-17)*

Sabbath is a sign, a signal between God and us. When I played baseball, we had signs: fastball, curve, changeup, steal, bunt, take the next pitch. The sign existed as a way for the coach to instruct the player what to do next. To ignore the coach's sign was the quickest way to sit on the bench. In Exodus, God sends a sign to Israel. After six days labor, God calls for a day of rest. This is somehow connected to our sanctification: "You shall keep my sabbaths, for this is a sign between me and you throughout your generations, given in order that you may know that I, the LORD, sanctify you" (Exod. 31:13). God cannot make us holy without our participation in the rhythms of grace.

There is no command to sleep, because we cannot violate the sleep/labor patterns without crashing. But we can violate the 6/1, 6/1, 6/1 pattern. Our bodies won't shut down for a while. It is physically possible to live out the pattern 7, 7, 7, 7 until we fall dead. The Jews had a name for people who did this—slaves.

God never intended us to live this way. God is not a slave driver. God liberates His people from slavery. We are more than the work we do. We are meant to be defined as creatures of a loving God. Work is what we are given to do in partnership with God in His creative enterprise in the world. Sabbath is part of the process. It includes meaningful, rested worship of God. In this act, we re-center our lives as a community of faith on the God who is our life. Sabbath involves family and friends. We eat together, slowly, and linger at the table to talk. We take long walks. We play together. We take naps, read novels, paint pictures, ride bikes, visit neighbors. I think the last thing God wants from us is some pious performance of avoiding life's restful joys. God is re-creating us!

As with most good gifts, we humans messed up the gift of Sabbath. This gift of law was hamstrung with rules and regulations that made the day more about what we could not do than celebrating what we were invited to do. Some of Jesus' sharpest conflicts with religious leaders were over Sabbath. Don't travel on Sabbath. Don't pick grain for a snack. Don't heal the sick. The Sabbath became a burden rather than a gift. In Jesus' view, people were not made to be crammed into the Sabbath regulations; Sabbath was given as a gift of God to tired people.

Can you dance with this law? If you continue living at the same pace you are now, will you like the person you become in ten years? What is the quality of your life off the clock? Can you relax? Do you know how to stop working? When, during the week, does God's grace penetrate your fatigued spirit and invigorate your life? When do you get still and hear the whispering God? When do you recalibrate, recharge your soul batteries? When do you really play?

It is interesting that the Ten Commandments, when viewed in the context of the Babylonian exile, are placed side by side with Isa. 40—55. These chapters contain some of the loftiest scriptures about creation in the Bible. The people who long for liberation are being reminded that the creative work of God, begun in the formation of the world, is ongoing. God is still creating. Sabbath is the central reminder of this reality.

In the Christian faith, Sabbath is connected to the first day of the week, the day of resurrection. In a sense, our Sabbath is no longer the seventh day of the week, but eighth, or the first day of the new creation. At the end of this old dying world's best effort at being God, we find a fateful Friday, a tomb-ish Saturday, and a resurrection Sunday. We are now living out the new creation begun in the resurrection of Jesus. The future becomes possible, manageable, hopeful because Jesus is alive (again).

I think God hopes to catch us fully alive on Sunday,
>   worshiping with our whole heart
>   photographing a fall tree resplendent in sunburst colors
>   bouncing a snowmobile over hills

cranking a stereo player with our favorite music and ly-
　　ing on the floor singing along
wrestling with kids in cool grass
laughing with friends on the back porch
running for a pass in the end zone
curled up with a good book
taking a nap while pretending to be interested in a foot-
　　ball game
embracing the love of our life
resting—just resting in the grace of God
or maybe, just maybe, dancing with the law of Sabbath

Remember the Sabbath
7th period was God's reservation
so it should be ours

Observe the Sabbath
Keep it Holy
Take set aside for God's purpose
work is not a physical effort
what would a day of rest from
work, look like.

HEAVY

Commandment 5

*Honor your father and your mother, so that your days may be long in the land that the L*ORD *your God is giving you.*
(Exod. 20:12)

Xtal – Brother Anniv,

each Day

The way we interpret the fifth commandment reveals our stage in life.

Children grow up with the verse, learning it at an early age in Sunday School. They are reminded of it by parents, youth workers, pastors, and other well-intentioned adults throughout the rest of their pre-childbearing years, but I don't think any of us ever get a grasp on what this commandment means until we have children of our own. Until we finally understand what our parents hopefully did for us and face that future of sacrifice with eyes wide open. So what the commandment means to us has a lot to do with how old our children are.

As a parent of young children who are often squirmy and sly, the commandment means obedience, pure and simple. Do what your mother and father tell you to do. Share your toys. Don't hit. Play nice. Eat your broccoli. Pipe down. Don't ask Mom for what Dad said no to and vice versa.

As the parent of teenagers, the commandment means obedience without an attitude. Clean your room. Do your homework. No mouthing off or talking back. Respect our eardrums. Be home on time. Stay away from the bad stuff—alcohol, tobacco, premarital sex. Go to church. And in case the teen child thinks this isn't a serious command, we go to the next commandment, "You shall not murder," which allows us to do anything short of murder. If this doesn't work, we read the texts from Exod. 21:15-17, which do permit murder for cases of cursing and striking parents. If you add Deut. 21:18-21, we get to invite all our friends to come help with the stoning of our teen child.

As parents of college students, the commandment means doing the right thing when we're not there to make you do what you already know you ought to do. It means making us proud of you by not wasting the hard-earned dollars we are investing in your college education. It means calling home occasionally and, when you come home on break, sitting at the kitchen table and talking to us for a few minutes before running off to meet up with all your old high school pals.

As parents of married adult children who have borne our grandchildren, the commandment means coming to our house for Christmas as soon and for as long as you can. My wife has perfected the art of getting the kids home for Christmas. She buys elaborate gifts and lets all the kids know they're at our house under the tree. She tells them they're welcome to come get their gifts before the stores open for return items on December 26. Just kidding. The commandment also means letting us spoil the grandkids, as well as respecting all we've learned through the years. A few sips of our sugary coffee won't kill you.

As a parent approaching retirement, it means picking up the check at the restaurant for us, mowing our lawn on hot days, and rubbing our sore backs while praising us for doing a wonderful job of parenting. You are also welcome to repay the college tuition, the wrecked-car cost, and the price of the wedding—as an act of respect for your soon-to-be-without-income parents.

As an elderly parent whose spouse has recently died, who is now wilting away in the nursing home, it means, "Come see me!"

This commandment is the most revealing of our character and quality of life on earth. One never ceases to be a parent or child. Even as we age, these definitive words remain descriptive of the relationships that define us. The parent-child relationship is one that moves from power to weakness. The parent, who begins powerful, ends weak. The child, who begins in utter weakness, ends powerful. At the beginning, I, the parent of a puking, pooping baby, am all-powerful over this tiny creature of fragility and weakness. I hold responsibility for this little one's life in my hands. I can care or not care, teach or not teach, bless or curse. What I do forms the life of this child.

But as time passes, the child takes the form I have exemplified and, for better or worse, becomes an adult. Apart from divine corrective grace, the child probably reflects me. I age, grow weaker, older, and less powerful. If I live long enough, I become the puking, pooping weak one who needs to be changed, fed, and cared for. And my child is potentially the only person in the world with a bond strong enough to responsibly care for me.

What I did with power to my child returns in his or her response to my weakness. What goes around comes around. Life has run full circle. Maybe that's why we plead the fifth commandment. Can you hear it? The whispered "please"? "Honor your father and mother . . . please!"

The context of the Exodus story is concerned with future generations remembering the miracle of liberation. It is written with an invitation for children to marvel at the way God creates a people from scratch. You find phrases like "when your children ask you" and "from generation to generation" scattered throughout the narrative. The fifth commandment instructs the young, yet mature, adults with aging parents to honor their mothers and fathers so that their lives in the land will be long.

The word *honor* is *kabad*. It means the same as the old hippie expression "Heavy," which meant serious. The Hebrew word actually means "heavy, gravity, importance, significance, to be taken seriously." It is the polar opposite of *qalal*, which means "lightness, slightness, and insignificance." These polar pairs are often used in the same sentence in the Old Testament. God honors *(kabad)* those who honor Him but despises *(qalal)* those who treat Him in contemptible ways.

To take the parent seriously and to respect the gravity of his or her presence could mean several things. Primary among them in the Exodus context is to listen to the stories he or she tells. The parents have seen the activity of God and are shaping the next generation by telling the stories. There were no personal journals, videocams, or tape recorders in the wilderness. As they circled waiting for a generation to die before entering the Promised Land, the stories were being buried along with the parents.

Unless the young respected the words of the dying generation, the narrative of the God who brought His people out of the land of Egypt would be soon forgotten. Unless they listened to the stories and understood their weight, they would soon be rootless nomads without history who did not know the God of Abraham, Isaac, Jacob, and Joseph.

Honoring the parent also has something to do with identity. In America, we define ourselves as individuals. Our cultural definition of a person would be

I am an individual.

I am distinguishable from you.

I have a social security number that is different from yours.

I exist in this identifiable skin sack.

I make choices in line with my ruling desires.

I enter relationships that are meaningful to me.

I seek out experiences that are relevant to me.

I have limited time and do not want to waste it on uninteresting people.

I am not obligated to you unless I choose to be, and you have no right to expect anything from me unless I give you that right.

I am responsible for myself, for only myself.

Does something about that definition seem a little off? Maybe our definition of a person is all wrong.

In the Bible, a person is identified not by his or her separateness from others but by his connection to others. An Israelite is a son or daughter of Abraham. Saul is named as one who belongs to the tribe of Benjamin. Covenants unite people and give them their identity. Personhood is not our radical difference from each other but our radical belonging to each other.

The biblical definition of a person would be

I am a child of God.

I belong to the parents who birthed me.

I belong to the people of God by baptism.

I exist as a body in a body.

I take interest in the lives of my brothers and sisters.

I seek to be faithful to the ones I love and the ones who love me.

I am in relationships that are given. Some are energizing and some are draining, but they are all important.

I am obligated. People have the right to expect certain things of me in light of the covenant that exists between us.

I cannot think of myself apart from them.

I am a new creation of God by way of the narrative of liberation.[5]

To take our parents seriously, to honor them, is to recognize that our own identity is rooted in them and that our very name, body, and breath are their doing. "Honor is a delicate, transactive maneuver, whereby both parties grow in dignity through the process."[6] Bonds of this sort are the kind of rope that can tie a family, a clan, a community, a people, a nation together. It's no wonder the commandment suggests that those who honor the parents in these ways will live long in the land. In a nomadic world, the clan would be strong, the stories formative, the ground holy, the bonds sacred, and the land passed down from generation to generation.

If parents can be easily dismissed or discarded, then we each define ourselves without the vote of our ancestral history. Our self-made story eliminates and trumps all previous ones. It's as if nothing important ever happened until we came along. We take credit for our successes while blaming our parents for all our failures. The past has no claim on us. Our parents do not live on in us. They are insignificant, weighing almost nothing, and our bond to them is certainly not heavy.

It may be that the second context of the commandments, the Babylonian exile, has even more to say in our understanding of the fifth commandment. Could it be that the people find themselves in exile because they stopped listening to their parents?

They forgot who they were. They developed amnesia for lack of a formative history. They lost their guiding narrative. They cannot get home because they have forgotten the way. They are no longer living long days in their land but are slaves once again in another's land.

Exodus is being recalled to remind them of the basic structure of covenanted life that got them through a wilderness into the Promised Land. They must gather the elderly, listen to the stories, and remember their God who hears the cries of exiles. This is the way back. The commandment calls upon them to cease all action that denigrates the elderly parents.

When we view life as something that can be discarded, especially the lives of those who give us our identity, we are on a dangerous path; we are on the way to exile. If our elderly parents can be easily dismissed, how much easier does it become to dismiss life in the womb, the poor on the streets, the starving in other countries, the imprisoned, the dying? Once we learn the art of dehumanizing the sacred creatures of God, we have little time left as a bonded community. Some power will seize us and treat us as we have treated each other. And who is left to care when everyone is looking out for self?

"Hear, my child, your father's instruction, and do not reject your mother's teaching" (Prov. 1:8).

"A fool despises a parent's instruction, but the one who heeds admonition is prudent" (15:5).

"Those who do violence to their father and chase away their mother are children who cause shame and bring reproach" (19:26).

Honor them. Listen to them. Say thank you. Call them and express your appreciation for their sacrifices. Tell them you love them. Visit them. Include them on holidays. Gather the family to hear their stories. Fix their house. Handle their legal issues. Hug them. In fact, go ahead and dance with them.

10
LIFE IS SACRED

Commandment 6

You shall not murder.

(Exod. 20:13)

The following is a true story of great loss, as told by Mika Moulton, the mother of Christopher Meyer.

Christopher arrived in this world a whopping 10½ pounds. He was a happy baby and even happier toddler. As he grew, he developed a compassion and understanding of others and an even deeper caring for animals. He could make friends with anyone or anything.

In 1995, Christopher was 10½ years old. We lived in the small village of Aroma Park, Illinois. Like any young boy with adventuresome blood, he loved the riverfront. There were intriguing things along the river that could set a young boy's heart pounding and his mind soaring. Around noon on August 7, 1995, Christopher asked me if he could ride his bicycle two blocks down to the river with the other neighborhood children. I told him that he could go, but to be back by 5 P.M. Christopher said he would be home on time and rode off. When he hadn't returned home on time, I went to the park by the river and searched for him. Finding no sign of him, I contacted the county sheriff to report him missing. After speaking with other adults and children in the park and along the riverfront, it was discovered that they had seen Christopher talking to a strange man before leaving the area to ride home. An immediate search began by the county law enforcement, local fire departments, as well as the search and rescue dogs.

Two days after his disappearance I was called down to the fire department. There was a glimmer of hope that raced through my body as I imagined his toothy grin and pale blonde towhead sitting there waiting to see me and then my nightmare would be over. However, my need to be summoned to the fire department was because a bike was found, hidden among some trees and brush across the river. They asked me to identify it as Christopher's. I sank to my knees, realizing that the bike was his with its muddy tires and broken speedometer. Then, moments later, a diver brought in one of his shoes. It was found floating in the river about a mile downstream. The following day his other shoe was found 4 miles downstream. Pieces of his clothing were found in a wooded area about 20 miles away.

Within two days of Christopher's disappearance, the county sheriff received information that a recently released murderer was living in a nearby city. His name is Timothy Buss. He had grown up in the area. He had been in prison for murdering five-year-old Tara Sue Huffman in our community in 1981. Buss was 13 years old at the time but was tried as an adult. He had been found guilty and sentenced to 25 years in prison. He was paroled after serving 12 years of the 25-year sentence.

The police staked out a motel after a clerk called in a tip when she realized that a man that just checked into her motel looked like the composite sketch. The following day they watched as Buss placed his boots in a dumpster and followed him as he drove to another area of the river and began talking to yet another boy. The police asked to talk to him at the station and he agreed, following the police car back into town. He allowed a search of his car, and the police found that the carpet in the trunk was soaked with blood. He was arraigned the following day. By now Chris had been missing for four days.

As each second ticked by it seemed like an eternity. I vaguely remember staring out my windows, watching the neighborhood children on their bikes. I wanted to run after them, screaming for them to get back in their houses, not to be out in their yards playing. Didn't they realize how dangerous it was? And why were they happy? How could anybody laugh or joke or smile? My entire being was consumed [with] making the pain go away. I kept thinking, "When was I going to wake up?"

After over seven days of searching, with media trucks parked in front of my house, 15-20 coworkers and friends at my house all day long, and grasping for any tidbit of information available, I was exhausted. I finally accepted that this event in my life was bigger than anything that I could control. The searching had taken a toll on the police, fire fighters, and entire community. After the last person left my house that night, at about 1 A.M., I went to my bedroom, got on my knees, and prayed like I have never prayed before. I really felt like I was talking directly to God. I told Him that I could accept whatever He had in place. I told Him that it was time that I let Him take control and, again, I would accept the outcome. I then crawled into bed, and the next thing I heard—at 3 A.M.—was the doorbell. The police came to tell me that they had found a child's body.

On August 15, 1995, eight days after riding his bike away from home, Christopher's badly decomposed body was found, buried in a shallow grave. He had been stabbed over 50 times. Buss was found guilty of killing my son and this time sentenced to death.

Once the terror and all-consuming grief had begun to subside, I knew that I couldn't just sit and wallow in self-pity. I was angry that my son had been taken in such a violent manner. I was angry that the justice system had let a monster like that out of prison. I was angry that I didn't at least get to say good-bye. I realized, though, that anger is a powerful energy. I decided to redirect that energy into something positive. Since the death of my beautiful son, I began a quest and demand for educational life skills to be taught to children.[7]

Years ago when a preacher preached on the sixth commandment, the applicable points of relevancy were looks that could kill, murderous words, and criminal attitudes. Today the stakes are higher. Many of us know people who have been murdered.

Had I been ordering the Ten Commandments, I would have placed this one last. It seems that this is the epitome of dehumanization, the end of a slippery slope of sin. I'd keep the first four in place, because the erosion of life is rooted in a blatant disregard for the God who gives life. If we can make our own idolatrous gods, use God's name to endorse our will, turn Him into our genie in the religious bottle, then we can desacralize the life God created. First, we erase the Sabbath pattern that is meant to remind us of our relation to God. Then we dishonor our parents who gave us birth, placing ourselves at the center of the familial universe. Next we break our promises to those we marry, then we take from others what is not ours, then we twist the truth for our purposes, then we want their life, then we take it.

In 1973, we crossed a moral line that has legally legitimized the taking of life. With concern for the living who have experienced the consequences of abortion, and with mercy toward those affected by it, we cannot underestimate the weight of this national choice. It seemed such a simple thing—keep women from unsafe, deadly abortions by providing safe ones in certified medical clinics. It would be private and personal, based on the free choice of a free being concerning her own body. What began as a personal choice is now a standard method of birth control. Millions of infants have been terminated in the womb before ever gulping the first breath of the God-given air their lungs were made for. An industry of death now exists. To take the life of the unborn is the beginning of societal evil.

Just as American slavery was the blight on the conscience of a nation that led that nation to Civil War, abortion is the kind of choice that legitimizes the taking of any life that becomes inconvenient or unwanted. Just as Hitler's regime dehumanized the Jews and Gypsies as a prelude to their extermination, we are dehumanizing life as a rationale for ending the life of the unborn. It is not far from abortion to the mercy killing of the diseased to the destruction of babies who have inconvenient diseases or deformities. From there, we go to the poor or to those who can no longer work or to the minorities. Our culture has become coarse, disrespectful, impersonal, and brutal. Life is no longer a right but a relationship of power in which another has the say over the life of the weak or unwanted. Other nations have already taken the lives of tribal neighbors simply because they were ethnically different. We cannot kill our babies and then expect everyone to have a high regard for life.

Murder has become prime-time entertainment; we eagerly await the next episode of *Law and Order, C.S.I.,* or *Bones.* Murder heads the evening news and headlines the morning paper. Science works on the newest fatal biological viruses. Terrorists seek weapons of mass destruction. The military invents more deadly killing machines. Our society has become a culture of death.

Why have we moved in these directions? Could it be that in our violation of the first three commands we have made ourselves to be gods? As our own gods, we resist the limits and bristle at the law that makes us responsible for each other. We are drunk on our own thinking and numbed by our deadly ways. If we can rationalize it, we believe we can do it. In seeking to rise above our dependent humanness, we have violated the creaturely limits imposed on us by our Creator. God is saying that the murder of a person is a movement toward the death and destruction of the created order. It is a god-less move, an un-human act, a de-human deed.

Having suggested a high value on life, I must also add that preserving life is not the highest good. We are not called to sustain life at all costs. The person whose time has come need not be artificially kept from death by machines. There are causes for which it is right to lay down one's life. There are pregnancies that endanger the life of a mother that call for wise counsel. There are those killed in the line of protecting and serving others.

The command calls us to take a fresh look at the ways of our world. However, we will never make headway by condemning the world. It has enough deadly condemnation already. We are called to be the people of life. Our rampant, exuberant celebration of life is our response to its Gift Giver. As we dance with this law, our mind-set will change. We will see birthdays as benchmarks of grace, marriages as God's vote that the human race continue, meals as sacred conversations of the living, cemeteries as story vaults of God's interaction with his wildly varied creatures. We will play with children, listen to the elderly, care for the sick, feed the hungry, visit the lonely, help the weak—because God gives us life and means that we cherish it. Maybe we will watch fewer murder shows, vote for a lower military budget, oppose capital punishment, adopt a child, open our homes to a foster child, or regularly visit a retirement home. Or maybe, like Christopher's mom, we will refuse to let death take over our lives, and we will work to make neighborhoods safe for everyone rather than moving into a gated community.

11

A DECENT PROPOSAL

Commandment 7

You shall not commit adultery.

(Exod. 20:14)

Country music is arguably the most raw and most honest of the musical genres. And when it comes to adultery, the songs never end: "You Picked a Fine Time to Leave Me, Lucille," "Ruby, Don't Take Your Love to Town," "Your Cheatin' Heart." As you can see, my country music repertoire is somewhat dated. But there are new ones: "Before He Cheats," "Red High Heels," "Stay."

The heart needs a way to deal with the extraordinary hurt of a relationship gone wrong. As cute and clever as the songs are, this sin is no laughing matter. Like a single rock thrown into the pond, adultery sends ripples of pain in every direction—the spouse who felt cheated and cheapened, the child who felt the brunt of a parent's indiscretion, the parents of the adulterer, the in-laws muted and hurt, the friends of the couple, the future spouse of the child affected by example, the resolution of the relationship with the other party, and the burden of the adulterer. These ripples do not stop at the edge of the lake. Sometimes they become the tsunami that flattens a marriage and tears a family apart.

As sensitive as we are about human pain, you'd think our cultural leaders would be putting a stop to this tragedy. You'd be wrong. Affairs are everywhere, even reaching as high as the White House. Adultery has infiltrated our marriages, our entertainment, our society. There are an abundance of Web sites that offer tips for having a successful affair, give ready advice on how to cover your tracks, and show how having an affair can actually save your marriage. Really?

I realize I have the home field advantage of calling adultery a sin in a Christian book, most likely being read by Christians. Place me on a talk show today, and I'd be booed and hissed for suggesting that marital faithfulness is the primary covenantal bond for the human family and should be championed as the way marriage is meant to work. I'd hear about the scientific discoveries on the male need for multiple partners, the boredom in marriage that is often improved by mutually agreed-upon affairs, the innocence of momentary flings that were not intended to hurt anyone, and the current statistics on the lack of marital faithfulness today. I'd be labeled old-fashioned, puritanical, repressive, legalistic, and judgmental and would probably be called a dinosaur.

Maybe a visit to a time long past would be helpful. The Jurassic Park of our narrative is the Garden of Eden. Adam has been created but is unfulfilled. Something is missing. The animal pairs suggest to him a loneliness that cannot be fulfilled in the zoological parade. So, in response, on the sixth day, God created a stunning new creature to live in union for life with Adam; she was called woman. I think the sixth day may have been the epitome of God's handiwork. When the Lord presented her to the man, I believe a holy hush fell on creation. Mystery rises in the words "bone of my bones and flesh of my flesh" (Gen. 2:23). And the Creator was pleased.

The storyteller of Gen. 1 narrates it like this. Notice how the pronouns go haywire. "'Let us make humankind in our image, according to our likeness. . . .' So God created humankind in his image, in the image of God he created them; male and female he created them" (vv. 26-27). "Let us make," "he creates"; "in our image," "in his image"—the plural and singular flow into each other. Either God is talking to himself or God is schizophrenic. Something strange and marvelous is happening here.

The God known as Father, Son, and Holy Spirit is imaging these two creatures with relational capacity. The relational God is creating relational creatures. The mystery of Three who are One is re-created in the mystery of two who become one. And the language is not contractual ("and God orchestrated a merger between the party of the first part and the party of the second part") or even legal ("by the power invested in me by the state of Jurassic"). It is biological. The two shall become one and they shall be one flesh (see 2:24).

When you dismantle flesh, the language is not the separation of assets and custody of kids. It is amputation, severed limbs, removal of organs. These two are bound together by God and are intended to stay that way. They are naked, and there is no shame, because they are one.

All is well until the snake shows up asking questions about an off-limits tree. "Did the Creator ssssay, really ssssay, that you must not eat from the tree in the center of the garden?" (see Gen. 3). For the first time in our story, the Creator is spoken of in the third person. God is not speaking, or spoken to, but is spoken about. God becomes someone outside the conversation of their life. Can He be trusted? What's behind this limiting command? The snake recasts God—from gracious Creator to boundary maker, from loving provider to fulfillment blocker. Adam and Eve opened wide and swallowed whole the dooming lie that the snake is selling. "The fat lady sang." "Turn out the lights, the party's over." "That's all she wrote." "Those were the good old days."

It gets ugly from here on. The marriage shows stress. "The woman *you* gave me, she made me eat it!" (see 3:12). They've learned to blame someone else rather than take responsibility for their sin. They hide. They cover up. No telling what they will do to each other. In rebellion, they are ushered from the garden without a reentry stamp on the back of the hand. The ticket window is closed. The Garden of Eden is a memory, a hope, a longing.

And how are we doing outside Eden? We are lusting after each other's bodies. Men are consuming pornography at alarming rates, perfecting the art of turning women into objects. Women are bitterly demanding equality on all levels and seeking to escape the domination of the garden curse. We are cautious, defensive, guarded. Maybe we are from different planets, like Mars and Venus.

Once, inside God's garden, we enjoyed erotic passion without shame. Now, outside the garden under our own management, we seek intimacy hoping to get out without getting hurt. Once we loved and cherished. Now we lust and use. Once we cared about each other's well-being. Now we seek our own individual pleasure. Once we were promise keepers. Now we are self-fulfillment seekers. Once we were one flesh. Now we are one-night stands.

After the mess we made, you would think God would be glad to be rid of us—"Hit the road, Adam and Eve, and don't you come back no more, no more." But God refuses to give up on His creation. God knows what we are capable of when we live in obedient relationship with Him and His power indwells us. The capacity for a God-resembling, God-honoring marriage still exists. God gives interesting gifts to Adam and Eve: clothes and commands.

The clothes replace the itchy fig leaves. Having picked figs in Mississippi, I cannot imagine wearing them; Adam and Eve must have wanted to cover up bad! Durable animal skins become the necessary fashion for covering their bodies. It isn't safe to go naked outside Eden, not because God is prudish (He opened the first nudist colony!), but because He saw what we could do to each other, how quickly we can reduce a person to naked flesh. Clothing curbs our desire to treat others as objects. Clothing protects us from people who would use us but do not love us. Clothing keeps us shielded until relational conditions make it safe to undress. So God gave us these personal body fences called clothes.

God also gave us commands, such as, "Do not commit adultery." Jesus, in the Sermon on the Mount, gets behind the command to the motive and forbids looking at a person with lust in the heart. Lust is the mental manipulation of another person for the sake of selfish sexual gratification. It is controlling another in our mind, undressing a person mentally, living in a perpetual sexual show with self as the star. Lust is passion without boundary or respect for the other person. And Jesus says, "No!" Not because Jesus is a prude, but because lust cripples our capacity to love as we were meant to love. Lust conditions us to objectify and use people, to take without giving, to demand without promise. If we perfect the practice of using a person, we will never be able to see that person with loving regard. A pawn is very different from a partner.

The question is asked, what is so wrong about sex outside marriage, single or married? God has rooted the marriage relationship in the physically expressed sexual practice of lovemaking. There is a celebratory bonding act at the heart of marriage. That adultery is primarily sexual calls attention to what we do with our bodies. (I would be quick to say that there is adultery that is not sexual, and just as much a sin.)

Sexual intercourse is more than a physical act. According to Scripture, it creates a one-flesh bond. Something of the spirit and being and body of one person attaches to the spirit and being and body of the other. When you sleep with a person, you can no longer see him or her through the same eyes again. It is an encounter between a man and a woman in which each does something to the other, for good or bad, which cannot be erased. You become an ongoing part of the person who walks away. Each gives something that cannot be taken back or voided. Sex leaves an indelible imprint. In Paul's words, "Do you not know that whoever is united to a prostitute becomes one body with her? For it is said, 'The two shall be one flesh'" (1 Cor. 6:16).

What's wrong with sex before and outside marriage? You are affixing something of yourself to the being of a person who is not committed to staying with you. And even more, you are learning to love and leave, or use and leave. You are practicing the deadly skill of bonding and breaking, bonding and breaking. You are lessening your capacity as a person to bond and stay bound, love and remain committed. One-flesh unity becomes cheap.

When I was a student at Trevecca Nazarene University, I worked the night shift at the Alamo Plaza Hotel. My shift ran from 10:30 P.M. to 7 A.M. I checked in late guests and did the night transcript of the business transactions of the day. I relieved an employee named Jerry, a grad student at Vanderbilt University. As he would leave the office, he would often say, "If you need me for anything, I'll be back in room [fill in the blank] with someone I checked in earlier." His goal was sexual conquest. In our office storage room, he had a little storage space where he kept the spoils of his conquest: panties. This went on for two years.

One night, Jerry came in the office at about three in the morning and slumped on the couch. "I don't get it! You've never slept with your girlfriend even though you're getting married this summer. I've had girls anytime I wanted. I'm so lonely. It doesn't seem right. I'm experienced and you're not. Yet I have no real friends in my life. Your friends come and go all the time. I'm jealous of the kind of friends you have." I replied, "Jerry, you are more experienced than I am, but not at loving. You have years of experience at using people, bonding sexually with them and then walking away. You've lost your capacity to love."

I've heard the arguments: "What happens between two consenting adults is nobody's business but theirs"; "Nobody is getting hurt"; "What I do with my own body is my own business."

Are we sure nobody is being hurt? What about the four hundred thousand babies born to teens each year in a permissive culture, over half of whom will live in poverty? What about the 1 million abortions each year? Or the 65 million people living with a sexually transmitted disease? What about AIDS? Or middle-aged women traded in coldly by their husbands for a younger model? What about the kids affected by divorce? What about friends you can't look in the face? What about ruined pastors, teachers, leaders? What about when your kids come to you and ask, "Did you?" We're not hurting anybody? Get real. We're killing each other with our immoral sexual behavior.

I recently wrote a letter to a friend. He was having an affair and asked my counsel. The names/details are changed.

Dear friend,

I'm glad you are meeting with a Christian counselor. She is a skilled professional and will serve you well. Here's my advice.

If you can find the energy to reinvest in your marriage to your wife, you will offer your family and friends (especially your children) a model of courage and faithfulness that will serve them the rest of their lives. This will mean that your heart and mind trump your emotions for a period of time as you take the hard and awkward road of restoring a broken relationship. It will be much easier to walk away and into the next relationship, but you will have formed in your heart the capacity of leaving someone. Having said this, I don't know how much energy you or your wife have left in the tank. To do this, you will need professional help. Your wife will have to want this, even in her deep hurt. There will be setbacks along the way as each of you work through it. My experience is that couples who get serious eventually find their feelings for one another healed and restored.

Five years from now, you will be glad you did this—at Christmas, family reunions, graduations, births of grandchildren, deaths of each other's parents, etc. God usually asks us to do the hard thing first and then comes reward. The easiest path is usually downhill.

As for the person that you've been involved with, you will grieve the loss of a relationship that has been an escape from the pain of a marriage that has not been fulfilling. Don't underestimate the pain of the grief, but you cannot afford to nurse the grief with an occasional fling. There would have to be an accountable end to the relationship. Your friends—and you have some good ones—will need to look you in the face once a week and ask you if you've seen her, talked with her, or been with her. Are you really ready for that?

I know you have questions about getting to heaven. I will not presume to answer for God. I don't think we humans are called to decide someone's eternal fate. But my concern is not getting you to heaven, but getting heaven into you. Can you begin, even now, to participate in the resurrection of Jesus—that which is dead being brought back to life by the power of a God who can raise the dead?

There are men all over the world who have left their wives for another woman. This is easy. Staying in a marriage that is broken, and working to make it good again, is hard. Is it in you, by the help of God, to do this?

One other thing, you may be able to take this road, and your wife may not be able to walk it with you. She has as much to say about the future as you. My guess is that her heart has hardened toward you. Both of you will have to decide to be restored.

If it is not possible, divorce is God's allowance to keep you from continuing to destroy each other. But I've always believed two processes should not be entered into prematurely—divorce and embalming. Don't end something that God is not done with. God will not abandon you, nor will I.

Blessings,

Dan

As we go forward in a world where adultery is rampant and sexuality is anything but what God intended it to be, I have two prayers.

For our children: God bless our children. May they grow up in homes and learn to love the God who establishes covenant with us. May they be given a healthy understanding of their sexuality. May they see Dad and Mom love each other with joy and grace. May they find security in who they are to buffer them against the tumultuous teenage years. May they respect boundaries. May they fall in love with one who is renewed in God's image and likeness. May they know in marriage the beauty and fulfillment of sexual intimacy. May they find strength to weather the storms of life and be drawn closer in the hard times. May they be faithful until death parts them.

For the broken: May the pain and hurt of adultery drive them into God's arms. May they stop resisting God's ways and open themselves to Him. May they ask forgiveness and be forgiving. May they stop destroying themselves by debilitating practices that cripple their capacity to love. May they respect those to whom they have made promises, and stop using those to whom they have not. May they draw a decisive line and walk away from sin. May they be restored by repentance, healed by grace, and guided by the Spirit.

12
TAKERS AND GIVERS

Commandment 8

You shall not steal.

(Exod. 20:15)

The first heist happened in the garden. Two people—a man and a woman—with no previous arrests took fruit from a forbidden tree. The investigating officer said the theft made no sense. The couple had practically controlled the wealth of the known world. They were neither hungry nor needy. They lacked nothing. They had no reason to take fruit from the only tree placed off limits by the Creator. The two were in a partnership with God. They were caretakers of the garden, recipients of its produce. Different from the animals, they were created with tending capacities, the urge to wisely oversee and take care of creation. God had created them in His own image and likeness, with the capacity for four primary relationships—to God, to each other, to themselves, and to created things. In these relationships, we define what it means to be human.

They violated the first relationship by listening to the serpent and believing the lie that they could be their own gods by eating of the forbidden fruit. In raiding the tree, they revealed their desire to rule rather than be ruled. They preferred to be as God, knowing all good and evil, becoming the Creator rather than creatures. They were seizing sovereignty for themselves. The relationship with Creator was now bent inward on themselves rather than outward toward God.

They violated the second relationship by their treatment of each other, beginning with blaming the other for the rebellious act, then by the man naming the woman just as he had named the animals. This began the practice of man wanting to rule over the woman rather than honoring her as a helpmate in life. This was quickly followed by a murder in the first family as one brother coveted another. Soon the world was filled with *hamas*, violence—it washed over humanity much like the flood waters that would soon cover the earth (see Gen. 6:11).

The third relationship was violated when they sinned against themselves. They understood their identity apart from God. And the One who had lovingly created them became an objective other whose motives were to be questioned—or so said the serpent. Freedom under God became freedom from God, and they recast themselves as their own destiny makers.

The fourth relationship was violated when they seized the forbidden fruit as an act of ownership rather than stewardship of God's creation. They no longer respected the boundaries set forth by the Creator but would take what they could as a way of life. This was an affront to the divine-human relationship. And if they can do this to God, no telling what they can do and will do to each other.

In the creation of the new community, Israel, God gives them a simple command. Do not steal. Respect established boundaries. Return to the owner what does not belong to you. Power is not the privilege to take what you want. Scales and balances must be fair. Treat each other as God wished to be treated in the garden—His boundary respected, His ownership recognized, His creation tended, His gifts appreciated. Honor the property of others. Respect ownership. No stealing.

It matters to God how we relate to things and how we relate to the people whose things they are. God, having experienced a garden robbery, knows what theft feels like. And He knows what it does to His creation.

None of us wants to live in a place where theft is the way of life. Africa has seen the horror of ethnic cleansing that permitted one tribe to take from another their belongings, land, and life. Moscow has seen the transition from Communism to democracy stalled by the presence of the Mafia, who help themselves to the hard-earned income of the people. In Cuba, people surrendered to Castro whatever he wanted. In America, our government flexes its strong arm of wealth and military power to get what we want. There are places all over the world where stealing is the way of life. Iron bars cover windows. Electric surveillance systems sell. Car alarms go off in the night. Deadbolts adorn doors. Guns wait in the drawers of bedside tables. Guards patrol the grounds. Gates protect property. Strangers are suspicious. These are places that suffocate the soul of God's free creatures. We were not meant to be eternally wary of each other's thieving intent.

I remember well the night my family was robbed. We lived in Raleigh, North Carolina, at the time. We had walked to McDonald's for ice cream with our two children. When we opened the front door, something immediately seemed wrong. I have come to believe there is a disturbance of the peace of a place when it is violated by theft. Denise's purse was gone from the counter. I looked to the left; the TV was missing with straggling wires hanging from the entertainment center. The back kitchen door had been kicked in. The doorframe was splintered. Our cats looked as if they had seen a horror movie. We had been robbed. Apparently, we had walked in on them because they had taken nothing else. They heard us and fled quickly out the back, across the creek, and into the neighboring subdivision. I slept by the back door that night while the rest of the family lay anxious in their beds. We had insurance. Everything was replaceable. But the theft went deeper than stuff. It was as if someone had said to us, "We don't give a rip about you, who you are, what you do for a living, what kind of family lives here—we just want your stuff." To be ripped off, robbed, stolen from is a dehumanizing experience.

The Israelites were well aware of this. They had been living in slavery for four hundred years. Pharaoh had been taking their lives from them—labor without pay, work without freedom, sweat without ownership. The cries of the people reached the ears of God and evoked from God a mighty deliverance. These landless people were guided to a land of their own, crops of their own, homes of their own—all to be tended under the law of God, which forbade theft and coveting. In their relationship to things, they were to be radically different from the people of Egypt.

In no way does our one night of theft place my family on par with the slaves of Egypt, or America, but it does cause me to think twice about how it feels to be robbed. When you cannot trust that people will respect your right to your property, you cannot rest easy. Peaceful existence is not possible where boundaries are not honored and respected.

The community of God is meant to be a place where we are not anxious about whether others respect our things. We are meant to be particular kinds of neighbors, employees, and citizens.

Are we?

- Office supplies taken home
- Long distance calls on the company line
- Company gas for personal errands
- Misusing the copier and postage meter
- Not returning our neighbor's shovel, ladder, or punchbowl
- Keeping library books
- Swiping hotel towels
- Billing for unnecessary services we perform
- Advertising wrongly
- Neglecting to pay the rent, mortgage, or car loan
- Denting a car and not leaving a note
- Withholding child support payment as an act of spiteful control
- Not reporting all the income on line 26, Form 1040
- Playing computer games while being paid by the hour
- Snacking on grapes from the produce section while shopping
- Stealing test answers with a glance
- Using more than our share of the world's oil, water, and air
- Buying goods made by people in sweat shops
- Plagiarizing a report
- Pocketing someone's spare change from the car cup carrier

- Walking away with a CD
- Selling a lemon for a mint
- Rigging bids
- Misusing copyright laws and legal loopholes
- Taking credit for someone's hard work
- Stealing a reputation with slander
- Smashing a kid's Halloween pumpkins on the front lawn
- Buying it, wearing it to the big dinner, and returning it
- Downloading and copying illegally

And that's the short list. I've gotten nowhere close to shoplifting, pickpocketing, safecracking, car theft, or common burglary. Theft rarely begins with the big stuff. It slowly encroaches, justifies itself, then dulls our conscience. That sneaky rationalizing voice sounds so convincing:

- "The government will only waste your tax money. Keep it for yourself and spend it on something better than they would."
- "The company owes you for all that overtime you put in. This is your way of getting even."
- "They overcharge at that store. It's time you evened the score."
- "Well, he still has my lawnmower."
- "It's just a library book, and I haven't gotten to it yet. They have public funds to replace these. My own taxes have more than paid for it."
- "I'm a lot more honest than that dealer, and if I don't make some money on the softies, I'll never stay in business."

Practices like these ultimately violate all four relationships. We disrespect God by offending His command. We disrespect our neighbor by stealing from him or her. We violate our own conscience by placing things above people. And we allow created things to become the dominating quest of our life. We are crippling our relational capacity.

It is time for us to bring our stewardship of the earth's goods under the scrutiny of the God who owns it all. If we can see someone else's stuff on a satellite or computer halfway around the world, certainly God sees all our stuff. God knows how we got it, from whom we got it, and whether or not our way of getting it was acceptable. God knows how we do business, how we treat customers, how we view people. God dismantles all rationalizations that harm His creatures and creation. And He says to us clearly, "Do not steal!"

Dancing with this law begins in our relationship with the Giver. We have to stop stealing from God. In Mal. 3, God is seeking to restore broken relationships with His people, but the restoration is impossible because they are ripping Him off. They are bringing their sick, scrawny animals to the Temple and offering them as a sacrifice of worship to God. They are sending a signal that they do not care about the quality of their relationship with God. They simply want to meet the minimal obligation by giving God what no longer has any value to them. In God's words, they are robbing Him. God responds by commanding that they bring the entire tithe into the storehouse. Tithing is the worshipful act of returning to God the first tenth of what you produce or make. The principle of tithing is rooted in the garden narrative. God asks that we honor that which belongs to Him. He set a boundary around the first tenth and asks that we respect the tithe as His by bringing it to Him as an act of worship. Regarding the tithe, God says, "It is mine. You honor me by returning it to me" (see vv. 7-12). Adam and Eve seized what did not belong to them. They raided God's tree. The people of Malachi's day were doing it again. The people of our day are stealing from God when we pocket His tithe as if it were ours, not His. How hard is it to have a loving, trusting relationship with someone you are ripping off? And if we can do this to God, what will we do to each other?

Why would a person rob God? Maybe he or she does not know God. If this is true, and if a person had no desire to know

God, then tithing is just bad math. One hundred percent beats 90 percent every time. Maybe the person has never been taught to tithe as a principle of worshipful respect for God. If tithing is just the way a church raises money, the meaning inherent in the act is missing. Maybe the person has grown calloused toward the commands of God and prefers, like Adam and Eve, to be his or her own master. He or she has gotten used to keeping, clutching, and grabbing for all he or she can amass as a sign of his or her importance in the world. The practice of tithing is one of the surest ways to keep the eighth commandment.

It is also possible that our motivation for work needs a divine overhaul. Paul wrote to the Ephesians, "Thieves must give up stealing; rather let them labor and work honestly with their own hands, so as to have something to share with the needy" (Eph. 4:28). Our motive for work is that we might be givers, first to God who richly gives us all things, then to those for whom we are responsible, then to the neighbor as directed by God—local and global. We become givers through our work.

It dawned on me one day as a college student that I was a thief. I was staying up all hours of the night playing Rook. I was ignoring homework assignments and waiting until the last minute to cram for exams. I was passing my classes, but I was not learning how to be a good pastor. I sensed the loving God chiding me. I was stealing from the people I would one day pastor. I was stealing from them the sermons that I could deliver if I became a good scholar of the Bible. I was stealing from them the leadership I might offer if I would discipline myself. I was stealing from them solid and wise counsel by being a sloppy thinker. God had called me as a pastor to be a giver, and my work ethic as a student was forming me to be a taker. Our work ethic is another way we observe the eighth commandment.

We are made to be givers. It is not enough to refrain from taking what belongs to another. We are called to work in ways that meet the needs of those around us. This looks like financial giving, but it also looks like care for the elderly, environmental responsibility, social justice, and volunteerism. And it all flows from the gift of God beginning in the garden and anticipated in the fullness of the Kingdom to come. Because when God commands no stealing, there is a hidden promise beneath the command.

13

PIRANHA POND AND GOSSIP GRAVEYARD

Commandment 9

You shall not bear false witness against your neighbor.

(Exod. 20:16)

Communities are made up of people, and these people meet at conversation crossroads. Simply put, conversation crossroads are places where people talk and tell what they know. Bug a conversational crossroad, and you can detect the quality of life in that community. You probably know that God cares about people, but did you know that the conversations we have matter as much to God as the people we have them with or about? The apostle Paul zeros in on this issue in Eph. 4:29—5:2.

> Let no evil talk come out of your mouths, but only what is useful for building up, as there is need, so that your words may give grace to those who hear. And do not grieve the Holy Spirit of God, with which you were marked with a seal for the day of redemption. Put away from you all bitterness and wrath and anger and wrangling and slander, together with all malice, and be kind to one another, tenderhearted, forgiving one another, as God in Christ has forgiven you. Therefore be imitators of God, as beloved children, and live in love, as Christ loved us and gave himself up for us, a fragrant offering and sacrifice to God.

Can I condense those verses so you can more clearly see the commandments they contain?

- No evil talk out of your mouth
- No words that tear down
- No words empty of grace
- No gossip; no slander; no malice

I want you to come on a trip with me and visit two conversational crossroads. The first is Piranha Pond and the second is Gossip Graveyard. We'll examine the activity that goes on here, more specifically the kinds of conversations that take place. Let's travel first to Piranha Pond.

On the surface, Piranha Pond looks like your average recreational lake. You can swim in it, fish in it, and boat on it, but unbeknownst to the casual observer, this pond is deadly. It is teeming with deadly, ferocious fish, called piranhas. Piranhas are beautiful from the side, a silvery blue color. They are oval from tip to tip and flat and thin from gill to gill. Their average length is about the length of say, the human tongue.

From the side, piranhas might resemble a big, blue guppy, but from the front, you get a very different impression. Chances are though, that you'll never come face-to-face with one. You'll never see them directly in front of you until it's too late. And only then will you discover that they have very strong jaws and their teeth are like spikes, the bottom ones fitting between the top ones like shearing scissors. This gives them a strong grip and tearing power. Head on they aren't pretty to look at. They are simply effective and deadly.

I have a college professor friend in Nashville who keeps a piranha in his office. He tells me that when you isolate piranhas, they lose their aggressiveness. You see, piranhas usually travel in schools—piranha packs. And they team up to prey on the weak. When they see a floundering fish, they swarm. Any hint of weakness, any sign of vulnerability, any signal of struggle, and it's a feeding frenzy.

Living in community is tough enough for weak and injured people, but Piranha Pond isn't just tough—it's deadly. You may want to steer clear of Piranha Pond if you've recently been divorced or fired from your job. You'll want to stay out of the water if you don't measure up to the Joneses or if your self-esteem is fragile. And failure? The piranhas can smell it a mile away, so don't even stand on the shore if you've failed at something. Instead, you need to steel your emotions, seal your pain, smile through your tears, and suck it up. If you want to survive life in or near Piranha Pond, act as though you are in charge. No limping, no floundering, no vulnerability, and no failure, or you could be dead meat. It's sad what happens to people who live and work in Piranha Pond—they learn not to be genuine.

But maybe you're thinking, *That's not me; I'm not weak; I'm not a failure.* Well let me share another fact with you. Piranhas have also been known to attack the strong. And when they attack the strong, the bigger, the better. It doesn't matter how much money or power you have; meat is meat. It's the way of life down at Piranha Pond. They've been known to reduce a healthy person to bones in a matter of minutes. There are lots of skeletons at the bottom of Piranha Pond. The few who escaped the attack and lived to tell about it can show you their scars. Chunks of them are missing.

There ought to be signs posted around the pond—warning signs like "Piranhas live here." "Swim at your own risk." "Piranhas aren't picky—they just like blood." But unfortunately, there aren't any signs.

The scariest thing is that piranha ponds are everywhere. They're as small as two people with cell phones, a casual conversation over coffee, a front seat, a back room, a church lobby. And yet some of them are as large as a massive institution, a powerful corporation, a misguided country. Thanks to technology, the piranhas in the ponds are plugged in, hooked up, and networked. They send e-mail, they're on the Internet, they post things at the hospital, they make calls, they send letters, they schmooze and work crowds, they leave anonymous notes, they text—all because it makes their work easier and more deadly.

If you dare, go down to the pond someday and drop an underwater microphone in the middle of their conversations. You'll discover some fascinating things. Piranhas have instant recall of entire conversations. They remember and can reproduce perfect voice inflections. They can discern the motives behind words and the plots behind deeds. They will tell you not only what was said but also what was meant by it. They are clairvoyant.

Let me let you in on a little secret, though. For all their ferociousness, they're actually very insecure. Confront them and they'll back down. Get them alone and they lose their aggressiveness. They are actually sad little creatures with very strong jaws and a voracious appetite that they don't know how to fill.

They find security only in packs of those who think like they think.

The Piranha Pond—where often is heard a disparaging word, and the waters are bloody all day.

Come with me to a second place. Another conversational crossroad. It's called Gossip Graveyard. It's very quiet. Not even a whisper can be heard. It's surrounded by a fence, and no phone lines run in or out. Worn out news is buried there. Gossip is laid to rest. Words without constructive value lie six feet under. Take a stroll around Gossip Graveyard and read the tombstones. Each tells a story.

Here lies a rumor stopped dead in its tracks by the truth. I love the story behind this one. A new employee threatened a long-time employee. Rumors were started about how she got the job. A third party, a real truth lover, confronted the issue head-on and laid the rumor to rest.

Here lies the attack on the character of a godly man. This one is strange. A guy was in the wrong place at the wrong time and somebody tried to nail him—but his friends got to the bottom of the deal and cleared his name.

Here lies the last conversation with a former friend of loose-tongued persuasion. Wonder what happened there?

Here lies a dark secret, a past sin, confessed, forgiven, and forgotten. I bet a pastor put that one to rest. What that person did and repented of will go to the grave unmentioned by the pastor who helped a person make it right with God.

Here lies idle phone chatter. Two people decided to change their topic of conversation for the better.

Here lies a razor-sharp wit that had specialized in sarcasm. That one is easy enough to figure out.

The tombstones go on and on. *Here lies a buried hatchet. Here lies the chip on a shoulder. Here lies slander.* I love strolling through Gossip Graveyard and reading the inscriptions. How did this stuff get here?

The faithful patrons of Gossip Graveyard quietly brought them here and buried them and walked away. Oh, they could have taken this stuff down to Piranha Pond, thrown it in, made a big splash, and fueled the feeding frenzy. But they did the decent thing, the right thing, and gave it a decent burial.

The patrons of Gossip Graveyard get very little notoriety for their deeds. Most people will never know they knew. Most people don't even see that defining moment when they start to speak and are checked by a still, small voice, and gossip dies on the spot. But God notices and smiles.

The patrons of Gossip Graveyard get their kicks from seeing people walking around whole. They love seeing leaders who are respected, vulnerable people cared for gently, touchy situations handled face-to-face, and squabbles quickly settled. The patrons of Gossip Graveyard are also environmentally conscious—they dispose of trash when they see it. They safeguard the health of the community. They believe that every person is an image-bearer of God and by grace is capable of love.

And these patrons may be quiet, but they are brave. They've been known to wrestle a juicy piece of meat from the jaws of the piranha. They've even at times confronted piranhas face-to-face and have the marks to show for it. The patrons of Gossip Grave-yard are trustworthy.

- They are keepers of character.
- They are truth tellers.
- Their hearts are predisposed to love.
- Their words build people up.
- Their homes are safe havens.
- Their offices invite honesty.
- Their friends are real.
- They foster communities of caring.

And just as every community has a piranha pond, every community has a gossip graveyard. And the two places couldn't be more different.

The road we choose reveals our hearts. When God says, "Open your mouth and say *aaaahhhh*," He sees past our tongues, past our vocal cords. He sees our hearts. Our words are the windows of our souls. So God travels with us and offers to us a clear option and a healthy community. God is the forgiver of our sin, the guiding whisper before our next word, the sanctifier of our word-producing heart, and the custodian of community who hears each word we speak. God gets involved in our speech. He is concerned about what we say because He created the person we say it about.

The moment of choice, a defining moment, comes to all of us. We stand daily at conversational crossroads where we have two paths to travel, two destinations we can end up at. Piranha Pond or Gossip Graveyard. Where will we take what we know? What will we do with those meaty things called words? What kind of community will we build?

David
Barb

14
COVETING

Commandment 10

You shall not covet your neighbor's house; you shall not covet your neighbor's wife, or male or female slave, or ox, or donkey, or anything that belongs to your neighbor.
(Exod. 20:17)

Coveting is a marriage of two of the seven deadly sins—one part envy, one part greed.[8] Greed is the inability to say *enough*. It is the desire that lurks in the basement always asking for more. It is an emptiness that seeks fulfillment through the next acquisition. Envy is the inability to enjoy the life we have because our eyes and thoughts are always on what another person has.

Coveting weds the two by supplying the specific object of our envious greed—the neighbor's house, wife, slaves, or work animals. Coveting is worse than envy or greed in that it takes aim both at another named person and that which belongs to that named person.

Coveting is also rooted in the other commandments. Lusting after the neighbor's wife leads toward adultery. Wanting the neighbor's land and farm animals leads toward stealing. Making these persons and their objects the aim of our life is akin to idolatry.

The sin of coveting moves the commandments from deed to motive. It is possible to be covetous and never steal or sleep with the neighbor's wife. We simply want what our neighbor has. This heart hindrance makes it impossible to be a good neighbor. Coveting objectifies the neighbor and prohibits us from loving the neighbor as we love ourselves. It is a violation of community.

The last two commandments deal with the neighbor—not bearing false witness against the neighbor and not coveting what belongs to the neighbor. *Neighbor* becomes an important word for the people of God, and an even more important word in the double command of Jesus—love God; love the neighbor.

Now that I am a grandparent, I have been reintroduced to children's TV programs. I'm watching *Sesame Street* again. I've been away a long time. But I was pleased to see that not too much had changed. The people on the show were looking older, but the puppets had retained their youthful vigor. Elmo is more popular than ever and has been joined by some new friends. The Count is still teaching children to count and making thunder clap. And all of them are still singing my favorite *Sesame Street* song, asking "Who are the people in your neighborhood?" Remember that song? They talk about the daily tasks of the people you might rub elbows with on your street. The firefighter, the grocer, the mail carrier, and so on. It is a way of teaching children to know who lives and works in the neighborhood. And in my day (or at least my daughters' day), when *Sesame Street* was over, Mr. Rogers came on. This wonderful man began his show by asking, "Won't you be my neighbor?" He opens his home to the neighbors and introduces us to the people who live and work around him.

Children's television shows aren't the only ones who know community is important to us. Even the cell phone companies are interested in neighborhoods. They create a network of those who are on the "in" plan, meaning that they reside within the same carrier and can talk with each other free of charge. It's like a virtual gated community of cell phone neighbors. Some neighborhoods are as small as your favorite five. Others are as large as anyone on the same carrier. They are selling service by making it cheaper for us to be connected to the people we want to do life with.

God has always been interested in neighbors, because there was a time when His people had none. When they were slaves in Egypt and exiles in Babylon, they had no neighbors. There were no little Egyptian or Babylonian children walking around singing, "Oh, an Israelite is a person in the neighborhood, in the neighborhood, in the neighborhood. Oh, an Israelite is a person in the neighborhood, a person that you meet each day." They weren't on anyone's "in" plan. No one treated them neighborly. They were aliens, strangers.

And they cried. And God heard their cries and moved in love to redeem them from their slavery and from their exile. After God brought them out, He gave them instructions regarding neighborly love.

So now, O Israel, what does the LORD your God require of you? Only to fear the LORD your God, to walk in all his ways, to love him, to serve the LORD your God with all your heart and with all your soul, and to keep the commandments of the LORD your God and his decrees that I am commanding you today, for your own well-being. Although heaven and the heaven of heavens belong to the LORD your God, the earth with all that is in it, yet the LORD set his heart in love on your ancestors alone and chose you, their descendants after them, out of all the peoples, as it is today. Circumcise, then, the fore-skin of your heart, and do not be stubborn any longer. For the LORD your God is God of gods and Lord of lords, the great God, mighty and awesome, who is not partial and takes no bribe, who executes justice for the orphan and the widow, and who loves the strangers, providing them food and clothing. You shall also love the stranger, for you were strangers in the land of Egypt. You shall fear the LORD your God; him alone you shall worship; to him you shall hold fast, and by his name you shall swear. He is your praise; he is your God, who has done for you these great and awesome things that your own eyes have seen. Your ancestors went down to Egypt seventy persons; and now the LORD your God has made you as numer-ous as the stars in heaven. *(Deut. 10:12-22)*

The God who loves the stranger calls His people to turn strangers into neighbors by doing justice, feeding, providing, welcoming them into the community. In Egypt and Babylon, they did not experience neighborliness. In Israel, the strangers were to be loved. This love is rooted in the character and ways of God, who acted neighborly when no one else cared.

It is not often that we have the opportunity to experience being a stranger. My first trip to Moscow afforded me a moment to remember what that felt like. I had gone through the security checkpoints, immigration, and customs. I was to be greeted by someone bearing my name on a sign. When I exited customs, I saw no one bearing a sign with my name on it. I looked and looked. No one. I found a seat and began a long wait. It occurred to me that I had no Russian currency, no phone contact or knowledge of the Russian telephone system, no address to give to a cab driver. I was a stranger sitting in an airport where I didn't know the language. I was helpless. In that moment, God whispered to me, "Don't ever forget how this feels." Thankfully, after about an hour, my driver—and new best friend—arrived to take me to my destination.

Jesus met a young scribe who wanted to know the interpretation of loving the neighbor. "Who is my neighbor?" he asked. He hadn't seen *Sesame Street.* Jesus treated him to the parable of the Good Samaritan, where the neighbor ends up being the one who showed mercy.

This way of life—loving the neighbor, showing mercy, providing, welcoming—is the polar opposite of coveting. Rather than having an eye on the neighbor's wife, house, and work animals with the desire to have them, our eye is on the neighbor and our desire is to do him or her good. Where there is coveting, there can be no neighborhood.

EPILOGUE:
KEEP DANCING

It's been a long time since we stood at the foot of the thundering mountain and watched Moses return with stone tablets. We live in America, a place of individual rights. And if our rights as individuals are the priorities of our society and culture, we are doomed to be a land of lawsuits, power struggles, a privileged few, and huge prisons. It seems that civic responsibility and love for the neighbor might be a better principle to base our society on. After all, remember our defining story?

In the garden we grasped ultimate freedom to do as we pleased. And it yielded a man ruling over a woman, a brother killing a brother, and a world so bad that it drove God to hit the reset button and start all over again with Noah.

We don't do freedom well. When we try to dance on the principle of individual rights, we end up with two left feet. And no one to dance with.

If we aren't constantly learning, upholding, cherishing the law, we might just find that we are out of sync with our partner. We might even catch ourselves saying, "I'll sit this one out." And this would deeply trouble a God who gave us the law to help us. Believe me, He created us to dance. (Now would be a good time to reread Ps. 119, all of it.)

Happy are those whose way is blameless,
    who walk in the law of the LORD.
Happy are those who keep his decrees,
    who seek him with their whole heart,
who also do no wrong,
    but walk in his ways.

You have commanded your precepts
    to be kept diligently.
O that my ways may be steadfast
    in keeping your statutes!
Then I shall not be put to shame,
    having my eyes fixed on all your commandments.
I will praise you with an upright heart,
    when I learn your righteous ordinances.
I will observe your statutes;
    do not utterly forsake me.

. . . .

The LORD exists forever;
    your word is firmly fixed in heaven.
Your faithfulness endures to all generations;
    you have established the earth, and it stands fast.
By your appointment they stand today,
    for all things are your servants.
If your law had not been my delight,
    I would have perished in my misery.
I will never forget your precepts,
    for by them you have given me life.
I am yours; save me,
    for I have sought your precepts.
The wicked lie in wait to destroy me,
    but I consider your decrees.
I have seen a limit to all perfection,
    but your commandment is exceedingly broad.
    (Vv. 1-8, 89-96)

ENDNOTES

1. http://www.jesus-is-savior.com/Wolves/oprah-gospel.htm

2. Barbara Brown Taylor, "Preaching the Terrors," in *Leadership Magazine* (Spring 1992), 43. See the entire article for an excellent review of preaching biblical texts of terror.

3. Ibid., 44.

4. Ibid., 45.

5. These lists are adapted from my book *The Worship Plot* (Kansas City: Beacon Hill Press of Kansas City, 2007), 119-20.

6. Walter Brueggemann, *Exodus*, in *The New Interpreters Bible*, Vol. 1 (Nashville: Abingdon Press, 1994), 850.

7. Story by Mika Moulton, Christopher Meyer's mother. Permission to include story as printed here was granted by Mika Moulton. See Christopher's Clubhouse, http://www.christophersclubhouse.org, for an expanded version of Christopher's story.

8. I have written about each of these in the book *The Seven Deadly Sins: The Uncomfortable Truth* (Kansas City: Beacon Hill Press of Kansas City, 2008).

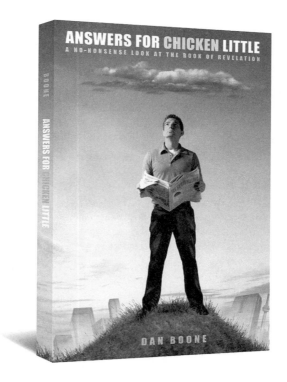

SIN. IT'S UGLY. IT'S DECEPTIVE.

IT'S THE ONE THING THAT KEEPS US FROM REALLY KNOWING GOD.

BUT TALKING ABOUT SIN MAKES US UNCOMFORTABLE.

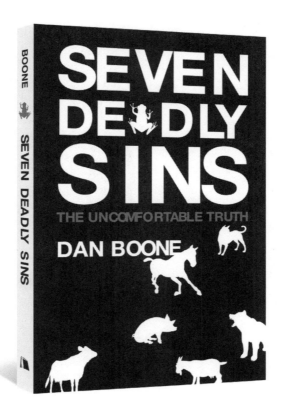

Seven Deadly Sins is a relevant, thought-provoking look at the seven imperfections that sin uses to tarnish and infect our lives. Written with compassion and understanding, this perceptive and challenging book will reshape your awareness of sin and remind you of a sin-free Savior who gives us the grace to become like Him.

Seven Deadly Sins
The Uncomfortable Truth
By Dan Boone
ISBN: 978-0-8341-2360-1

BEACON HILL PRESS
OF KANSAS CITY

Available online and wherever books are sold.